# Mae West

As Maudie Triplet in *Night After Night*, 1933.

# Mae West

## An Interview & Biography

### Clive Hirschhorn

Grand Cyrus Press
San Francisco

GRAND CYRUS PRESS, SAN FRANCISCO
www.GrandCyrusPress.com

© 2009 by Clive Hirschhorn
Second Edition 2010
All rights reserved.
Printed in the United States of America
and the United Kingdom.

ISBN 978-0-9790994-4-1
Library of Congress Control Number: 2009940560

Hirschhorn, Clive, 1940–
Mae West: An Interview & Biography
(West, Mae, 1893–1980)

Cover design by Ann Marra.
Cover photo of Clive Hirschhorn by ian cook.
Sheet music covers from the collections of
Roy Bishop and Harold Jacobs.

OTHER BOOKS BY CLIVE HIRSCHHORN:
*Gene Kelly: A Biography*
*The Films of James Mason*
*The Warner Bros. Story*
*The Hollywood Musical*
*The Universal Story*
*The Columbia Story*

# Acknowledgements

The bibliographical sources which I found exceptionally useful in the writing of this book were Maurice Leonard's *Mae West: Empress of Sex* (Harper-Collins, 1991); Miss West's own autobiography, *Goodness Had Nothing to Do with It* (W. H. Allen, 1960); *Mae West* by Fergus Cashin (W. H. Allen, 1981); *Mae West*, a biography by George Eells and Stanley Musgrove (William Morrow, 1982); and *The Celluloid Sacrifice* by Alexander Walker (Michael Joseph, 1966), *Becoming Mae West* by Emily Wortis Leider (Thorndike Press, 2001). To these books and their authors I owe a debt of gratitude.

I would also like to thank my supervising editor, Robyn Karney, for her assiduous work, and Eleanor Dugan, without whom this project would not have been possible, as well as Tom Vallance, Allan Lewis, LindaAnn Loschiaro, Pam Winter, and Photofest founder Howard Mandelbaum.

Clive Hirschhorn
London, 2009

In memory of my parents, Pearl and Colin.

# Contents

| | | |
|---|---|---|
| | Foreword by Leonard Maltin | ix |
| Chapter 1 | Meeting Mae | 1 |
| Chapter 2 | Learning Young | 13 |
| Chapter 3 | Mae the Playwright | 31 |
| Chapter 4 | Hooray for Hollywood | 43 |
| Chapter 5 | Hanging In | 71 |
| Chapter 6 | Ups and Downs | 95 |
| Chapter 7 | Bowing Out | 111 |
| | Index | 129 |

# Foreword

What has always struck me most about Mae West is that she was an absolute—and resolute—original. There has never been anyone else quite like her. Some people might point to Madonna as a show business figure who used sex in often outrageous ways to promote herself, but she hasn't Mae West's unique sense of humor about the world or herself. In the world of film, I can't think of any other woman who has created her own persona and crafted her own screenplays.

What's more, West's reputation has survived the decades. Young people might not know of her, but she is still widely quoted and referred to in articles and books. How many other show business personalities who flourished in the 1920s and 30s can say the same in the first decade of the 21st century?

Leonard Maltin

A Paramount publicity still, circa 1932.

## Chapter 1

# MEETING MAE

I do not remember exactly how old I was when I became aware of the existence of Mae West. Equally, I do not remember a time when this legendary Hollywood icon wasn't, for me, a symbol of everything that was glamorous and unattainable about the movies. There was something so unreal about her that she might have been made of celluloid rather than flesh and blood.

It hadn't occurred to me in October 1968, when I was in Los Angeles for my newspaper, the *Sunday Express*—and Mae was 75 years old—that she was still very much an active member of the human race. But a publicist with whom I had been working on a series of show business interviews suggested that it might be fun if I paid a call on Miss West. She would, he told me, probably give the interview in her boudoir, prior to which I'd be asked to lie down on her bed while she gave my arm muscles a

# Mae West

suggestive tweak. That's the way these sessions were usually conducted he assured me.

At first I thought he was joking, but he casually handed me her telephone number and address. She lived in apartment 611, the Ravenswood, at 570 N. Rossmore Avenue, Los Angeles, and had done so ever since her arrival in Los Angeles in the early 1930s. The address, I gathered, was almost as well known as its famous occupant. What he suggested I do was simply call her and make an appointment, adding, as if any additional encouragement were needed, that the great lady was extremely partial to Englishmen.

What could I lose? If it worked it would be something of a coup for my paper and a tremendous thrill for me. If not, well, at least I could say I tried. As soon as I returned to my hotel I made the call.

An operator at the Ravenswood answered. She took down some details, put me on hold for a moment then connected me with Miss West's apartment. A man with a rather effeminate voice took the call and, after feeding him the same details I'd given the operator, suggested I call at two o'clock the following afternoon when 'Miss West will be happy to see you.'

I could not believe it. Had it really been that simple to arrange? And although I was delighted at the thought of meeting the legendary Mae (or rather Miss West, as all her admirers called her) I was also a bit unsettled by her readiness to see the press. Could someone as famous as Mae West be so accessible and still retain her mystique? Well, I'd soon find out.

The following day I took a cab to the Ravenswood Apartments ('Doesn't Mae West live there?' asked the cab

## Meeting Mae

driver when I gave him the address). I took the elevator up to apartment 611, rang the doorbell, and waited. It was answered by an extremely well-dressed young man who invited me in. 'Miss West,' he said, 'is in a meeting with her lawyer. Please sit down.' Judging from his voice, it was the same man I'd spoken to the previous day. Also on the settee was another young man, immaculately attired in a grey suit, and a middle-aged woman. Fans, I gathered. Neither spoke to me—nor or to each other. The man who had shown me in disappeared, leaving me to sit with the other two visitors in self-conscious silence.

The room was carpeted in white and ornately furnished in gilt and ormolu. The walls were painted a very light yellow and on a reproduction French antique table rested an arrangement of begonias and roses—all artificial. In a corner stood a gold and white grand piano, providing a resting place for a nude statue, as well as for several framed photographs of Mae West. Dominating everything, however, was a nude portrait of the star showing her in her prime. Also depicted in the painting was a monkey, a species of which, as I later learned, Miss West was particularly fond. (She even used one in the opening montage of *I'm No Angel*.)

The young man who had shown me in, and who I subsequently discovered was just one of several adoring secretaries, returned to the drawing room and, without a word, walked over to a record player and put on a track from Mae West's latest LP—an album called 'Way Out West.' Seconds later he was miming to the disc—complete with all his employer's distinctive gestures. I don't think he was even aware he was doing it, it came so naturally to him.

## Mae West

This bizarre interlude ended with the song, whereupon Miss West herself, accompanied by her lawyer, sashayed into the room. She thanked her two silent visitors for coming to see her, autographed a couple of large glossy photographs for them, shook them both by the hand, and escorted them to the front door. The lawyer left without a word, and when I looked around I noticed that the secretary was nowhere to be seen either. It was just the legendary Mae West and I, alone in the apartment.

She was wearing a jet-black silk tea-gown that reached all the way to the ground, a blonde wig, and large black eyelashes. Her skin did not have a wrinkle in it—anywhere. For a woman of seventy-five she looked amazing and I told her so. 'Well, thank you,' she said, in that same seductive purr that thirty-five years previously had saved Paramount Pictures from bankruptcy. 'It's not how you look but how you feel. And honey, I feel as good as I look.' It wasn't one of her better lines, but it was a start.

She ushered me into her fabled boudoir. Dominating the room was an enormous bed with a brocaded canopy and a mirrored ceiling. 'Try that for size,' she said, and remembering what my publicist friend had told me, I assumed she meant the bed. Wrong. She was pointing to an ornate chair in the corner of the room. I sat down, feeling rather cheated that she hadn't seen fit to feel my muscles.

She offered me a drink—'Will a slimline Cola do?'—and, without pausing for my reply, continued, 'It had better, honey, 'cause I don't keep liquor on the premises.' She put one hand on her hip and, in the gesture that has helped perpetuate her image, lightly tapped her hair into place with the other. 'I have two vices. I don't smoke and I don't

# Meeting Mae

A glimpse of the legendary bed and ceiling mirror at the Ravenswood.

drink.' She disappeared for a moment, produced a diet Coke, sat down in a chair opposite me, and started to chat.

She told me that not even at the peak of her career in the mid thirties—with movies such as *She Done Him Wrong* and *I'm No Angel*—was she as popular as she was at the present moment. 'And you want to know why? I'll tell you in two words: Gla-Mour. I've still got glamour, honey, and the whole darn world is panting for glamour. They can't get enough of the stuff. I'm the epitome of sex appeal, and there's no use denying it. I started the whole thing, and I'm still Queen of the Roost. The only gal who came near me was pretty little Marilyn Monroe. And she was a sweet kid, too. But the rest of the gals? Big chests, small voices, and no brains.

'Glamour,' she continued, 'isn't just the way you look or the way you dress or undress. It's the way you think and feel. And as I thought and felt sex constantly, it was the most natural thing in the world that I should become a sex symbol. I was always sexy, but in a funny way the movies accentuated it. There were so many things we couldn't do in pictures because of censorship—like sit on a guy's lap—that I had to think of some gimmick or other if the story we were telling wasn't going to lose everything it had. So I developed my wisecracks, my walk, and my manner of speaking—and audiences flocked. And they haven't stopped flocking, if I may say so. It's the same all over the world. Even you refined Englishmen take to me. When I was there in 1947 with *Diamond Lil*, one of your big newspaper men, fella called Hannen Swaffer, said I was the greatest gal on two legs. Or words to that effect. Anyway, he liked me and as you know, he didn't like everybody!'

# Meeting Mae

She paused. 'It's like this,' she said, 'to the older fans I'm a nostalgic reminder of their past; of their courting days. I gave them some of the best times they ever had in the movies and they haven't forgotten. And the young people love me too because I personify the thirties and all its vitality. I stand for a good time in a world obsessed by violence. I didn't need Panavision and CinemaScope and color to help me woo the world. I did it with a gesture and an inflexion—and in black-and-white on a screen the size of a postage stamp. That's talent, honey.'

I suddenly noticed that the seductive purr with which I was greeted had disappeared. Her voice, as she went on, bore no traces of Mae West, the Hollywood icon, but was that of an elderly lady without affectation. 'Today whenever I make personal appearances I break records. The world is starved for talent and personality. Thank God I've got both. And I've still got my youth. As I said, only Monroe came near me in the sex stakes. The rest, like Jayne Mansfield or Sheree North or any of those other impostors, are just phonies.'

This reference to Jayne Mansfield immediately set her off on a tirade against one-time Mr. Universe, Mickey Hargitay, who had been one of Mae's hunks in her successful musclemen act in Las Vegas in 1954. Allegedly jealous of the affair Hargitay was having with Mansfield at the time, she 'demoted' him in the show by removing the few lines he had to say. Hargitay complained to the press and was fired. 'He told the papers I fired him because I was jealous of Mansfield and angry with him because he wouldn't sleep with me anymore,' she said. 'Can you believe that! I had my choice of some of the world's sexiest

# Mae West

W.C. Fields and Mae West in *My Little Chickadee*, 1940.

men. I didn't need Mickey Hargitay.' She suddenly stood up and, from under the cushion of her chair, produced a handful of yellowing newspaper clippings. 'It's all here. Everything he said about me. All the lies. I want you to go back to England and write the truth. Tell them that Mickey Hargitay needed Mae West much more than Mae West needed him! I mean, the thought that I could ever be jealous of that Jayne Mansfield. It's just too silly for words!'

Hargitay wasn't the only recipient of her vitriol during the hour-and-a-half we spent together. Ten minutes later she attacked one of her famous former co-stars, the great comedian W. C. Fields.

'There's a piece in today's *Hollywood Reporter* that talks about the several movies Fields and I made together. Well,'

# Meeting Mae

she said, 'we only made one picture together. It was called *My Little Chickadee,* and believe me, one was enough. The man was a drunk and I had a clause in my contract that said if I could smell alcohol on his breath he was to be kicked off the set. Which he was, often. So, how they can say we made more than one picture together beats me. As a matter of fact, I'd appreciate it if you'd call up the *Hollywood Reporter* right now and say you're a writer from England. Tell them that Miss West has asked for an apology. I mean, how *dare* they print such things!'

She meant it. The more she spoke, the angrier she became, and the next thing I knew, she was looking up the number of the *Hollywood Reporter* in the directory beside her bed. She found it, handed the phone to me, and asked me to dial. Somewhat nonplussed, I did and, deeply embarrassed, I found myself talking to the journalist responsible for the error and asking him to correct it. He said he'd see what he could do.

Miss West, who'd been hovering over me during the call took the receiver out of my hand and put it away. 'Good!' she said, *'that'll* teach them to print lies.'

At this point in our talk I needed to use the lavatory and asked where I might find it. She directed me to the bathroom and, on opening the door, I saw that the entire floor was covered in dirty towels and underwear. There was hardly any space that wasn't strewn with used garments, and I found myself gingerly picking my way through this minefield of soiled lingerie. When I returned to the boudoir, Miss West, who was suddenly looking much less glamorous than she had when I first arrived, and who had by now completely abandoned the sexy walk and talk, asked me if I

## Mae West

ever had any thoughts about extrasensory perception because, she said without waiting for an answer, she believed in it implicitly.

'I discovered the secret of inner meditation from a nun I once gave a Cadillac to,' she said. 'Oh, I'm always giving cars to nuns. Every year I buy a new model and I give the old one to a nun. I just can't stand to see nuns walking uphill or using public transport.

'Anyway, this nun told me how to find peace of mind through meditation, and I have. I commune with the spirit world and the spirits have helped me through a lot of life's problems. I'm a much fuller person for it, and a much more contented one. And it's helped me in my work, too. I once thought out an entire plot for a movie [*Every Day's a Holiday*] right down to the very last detail, in fifty seconds. It took me just fifteen minutes to describe it to the head of the studio, and a half-hour to dictate it to a secretary. The only proviso I had when the secretary was taking it all down was that I didn't want to see her hands so she wrote it under the table. Fascinating, don't you think?'

As our talk gradually wound down, I asked her the question I knew most women would like answered: how she managed to look so uncannily young.

'No secret,' she said. 'I go to bed early. I meditate. I eat all the correct foods, I don't smoke or drink, and I believe, *with a passion,* in myself. You can only beat nature when you show the bitch who's boss.'

That seemed an appropriate note on which to bring our meeting to a close, and, accordingly, I got up and thanked her for giving me so much of her time. 'Don't mention it, honey. You Englishmen are always *so* polite. It's a pleasure

# Meeting Mae

A publicity still, circa 1933.

# Mae West

to talk with you.' Suddenly the familiar Mae West intonations had returned and, as she escorted me to the door, so had the walk. 'Next time you're in Hollywood, why don't you come up and see me sometime...' I had been waiting for her to say it, and at last she had. Suddenly, framed by the doorway in her Ravenswood apartment, there was Mae West, the Hollywood goddess. For a time the myth had been submerged by reality and the legend had become little more than a vain and rather cantankerous has-been with failings and weaknesses like everybody else's. In that very last moment, though, the magic fleetingly returned.

If ever a star was the product of her own inventing, Mae West was top of the list. How, I wondered, did it all begin?

## Chapter 2

# LEARNING YOUNG

Mae West—real name Mary Jane West—was born on 17 August, 1893. At least that's what she admitted to, though it was not, of course, necessarily true. Indeed there is much about her childhood and formative years that is open to speculation, and it is often difficult to separate fact from fantasy. What *is* known, however, is that Mae's parents, John and Tillie West, had a daughter called Katie in August, 1891. The child died in infancy and, although no record of Mae's birth exists, it is likely that she was telling the truth when she admitted, in 1932, that 1893 was, indeed, the year of her birth.

Mae's mother, who was christened Matilda Delker Doelger, was born in Bavaria and emigrated to America in 1882 with her mother, her father Jacob, her two sisters, and two brothers. Though Jacob was a chemical engineer, a first cousin of his ran a brewery in New York, and beer became the Doelger family business.

# Mae West

Matilda, who was always called Tillie, hadn't been in New York for more than a year when, at the age of eighteen, she met and fell in love with John West. He was a colorful ex-featherweight prizefighter from Brooklyn (but 'of English and Catholic Irish descent' according to Mae) who was better known by his soubriquet 'Battling Jack.' The attraction was mutual.

A fighting man in more than just profession, Battling Jack was the quintessentially wild Irishman; a bellicose character who enjoyed nothing more than a punch-up and seeking out the company of attractive women. He drove around in his own 'carriage and pair' and, despite his streetwise manner, was an excellent raconteur. It was Jack's mother, Mary, who encouraged her son's romance, hoping that Tillie's influence, despite her family's brewery connections, would prove sobering and help Jack settle down in a steady job.

In 1885 Tillie—who earned a living modeling corsets (Mae called her a *'modiste'*), and who was also a woman of means—accepted Jack's offer of marriage. However, he did not settle down as his mother had hoped. After retiring from the ring, he became a bridle maker before eventually entering the racketeering business as a bodyguard to various underworld heavies in need of protection. He was certainly never short of ready cash.

Though Tillie was a practicing Catholic and regularly took part in church activities, there seems to be some confusion about her heritage. In Maurice Leonard's biography *Mae West: Empress of Sex,* Mike Sarne, who directed Mae in *Myra Breckinridge* (1970), is quoted as saying that Mae confided to him that her mother Tillie wasn't Catholic at all but

## Learning Young

Jewish, and furthermore, had taught her how to speak Yiddish. It was a family secret that had never before been divulged, she said. As Leonard points out, this would have made Mae West Jewish. Yet it was neither the Jewish nor the Catholic faiths that Mae embraced. She was, she always claimed, christened a Protestant in deference to her paternal grandfather who was Church of England. In the end, though, it didn't much matter. Mae's spiritual sustenance, as she herself said, derived from her belief in spiritualism and extrasensory perception. Religion hardly featured in her life at all.

As a child Mae's feelings towards her hard-living, hard-drinking father were ambivalent. She was fascinated by his manliness and by the world of the prizefighter that he came to symbolize, yet she hated him for his uncontrollable temper and the often cruel way in which he treated Tillie. Above all, she remembered hating the long black cigars he always smoked. She could not bear the smell, loathed it when he kissed her, and, as an adult, never allowed cigar-smoking in her presence. Alcohol was another strong dislike she carried into adulthood, never forgetting that her father was always at his worst after he had been drinking.

Because Tillie had secretly cherished unfulfilled ambitions of going on the stage, as soon as she recognized a flair for dancing in her daughter, she enrolled Mae, at the age of seven, in a dancing class run by 'Professor' Watts. An amateur Sunday night concert soon followed, during which the little girl threw a tantrum when she was denied a spotlight for her number, 'Movin' Day.' Amused at her precocious show of temperament, the stage manager pro-

## Mae West

vided her with one, and young Mae West went on to win not only the audience's unqualified approval but a gold medal as well. From that point onwards there was no stopping Tillie, whose faith in her daughter's potential was almost as great as Mae's subsequent belief in herself.

With each new appearance, Mae's repertoire of songs increased, and the following year, at the age of eight, she was even doing impressions of Eddie Foy and the great George M. Cohan. Because of her amateur status, however, the only money the child earned was what she took home in cash prizes, usually ten dollars a time. One of the most popular of these amateur showcases was the Gotham Theatre in Brooklyn, owned and run by Hal Clarendon of the Hal Clarendon Stock Company. Clarendon was so impressed with the perky eight-year-old that he offered her a juvenile spot with the company for eighteen dollars a week. Her first appearance as a professional performer was in a typical melodrama of the period called *Ten Nights in a Bar Room*—whose message about the evils of alcohol Mae and her mother misguidedly hoped would not be lost on Battling Jack.

Other roles Mae tucked under her belt during this time were Little Mother in *The Fatal Wedding*, Little Willie in the famed melodrama *East Lynne*, and Little Eva in *Uncle Tom's Cabin*. She also claims to have appeared on Broadway at the age of eleven in the story of a poverty-stricken family, *Mrs. Wiggs of the Cabbage Patch*. This has never been verified. (*Mrs. Wiggs* was eventually filmed by Paramount in 1934 with W. C. Fields.)

Mae also regularly appeared with the Alvin Reynolds Company, chaperoned either by Tillie or by her father, whose interest in the theatre, as soon as he realized his daughter's money-making potential as an actress, was growing.

The budding actress' education during this formative period was confined to green-room gossip and backstage banter. Her schooling was virtually nonexistent and what little tuition she had was given to her by Tillie who taught her the rudiments of German and French. At the age of thirteen—when she was considered too old to play juveniles and too young to play adults—she did, finally, enroll at a school in Brooklyn. But how long she was there, or just what she studied, has never been recorded.

The fact that she wasn't working didn't mean that she'd lost interest in the theatre. While at school in Brooklyn she took dance lessons with Ned Wayburn who would become instrumental in the staging of Florenz Ziegfeld's legendary revues. Dancing was never Mae's strong point and it is doubtful whether the fan dance Wayburn taught her was ever put to professional use. Mae West was no Gypsy Rose Lee, though Tillie resembled Gypsy's mother. Just as Mama Rose held back her daughter Louise in favor of Baby June, Tillie had very little interest in her other daughter, Beverly, and lavished all her attention on Mae. The difference, of course, was that Rose's underdog daughter Louise—who became Gypsy Rose Lee—grew up to be a far bigger star than June, who became June Havoc. Beverly West wasn't even in the running. As for their brother John, show business held no interest for him whatsoever. He was very much his father's son, similar in both looks and temperament. There was no sibling rivalry there.

# Mae West

Mae's voluptuous figure provides ample rebuttal to the later bizarre rumor that she was actually a man.

In 1909, at the age of sixteen, Mae had developed into an extremely sexy young woman who, even in her mid-teens, was aware of her own sexuality. After a break of three years, during which she concentrated on her 'education,' she longed to return to the stage. She was invited to become part of a double act with a comedian called Willie Hogan—playing a hillbilly girl to his Huck Finn—and accepted with alacrity.

In New York the bill was augmented by an accomplished 'eccentric' dancer called Frank Wallace. Though in no way conforming to Mae's physical ideal (she claims that, ever since her teens, the men who attracted her most were bodybuilders), Wallace, who had a slender physique, somehow appealed to her. They developed a friendship which, in turn, grew into a romance of sorts, much to the initial disapproval of Tillie. She did not want her daughter's career jeopardized by the constraints of domesticity.

Aware, even at an early age, of her daughter's interest in sex—though Mae insisted she was still a virgin when she married—Tillie decided not to forbid Mae's friendship with Frank. Indeed, the more Tillie saw of Frank, the more convinced she became that Mae couldn't possibly find him sexually attractive. His personality was not nearly as forceful or as appealing off-stage as it was on, and Tillie was happy to imagine that her daughter's interest in him would be temporary and, at the same time, prevent her seeing other more likely candidates for long-term romance.

She was right about Mae cooling off towards Frank, but wrong about other men. Though Frank remained in love with Mae and continued to see her, Mae was anything but a one-man girl. She dated several other potential lovers, one of whom she fell head over heels in love with and wanted to marry. Predictably, Tillie was horrified.

# Mae West

This was not what she had planned and, knowing that to forbid the marriage outright would only encourage her willful daughter further, she managed to persuade her to join forces with Frank in a double act. She convinced her that professionally it was a shrewd move, and stood to be a profitable one. Frank, of course, thought it was a great idea. And eventually Mae, who enjoyed show business even more than the company of men, agreed that her mother's suggestion made sound professional sense.

Tillie then persuaded her daughter and Frank to accept a lengthy tour that had been offered—thus imagining that she had removed Mae from the potential threat of marriage. What Tillie didn't know was that Mae would finish up married just the same—to Frank Wallace!

While on tour, Mae did indeed forget about the man she left behind. She did not, however, forget about sex, and despite her friendship with Wallace, continued to have one scandalous affair after another. She was advised by a singer in the company to find a husband just in case she became pregnant. Mae West's own account of the incident, which she gave to *Premiere* magazine, goes as follows:

'This woman kept talking to me about all the kissing with the men in the show. She went on and on about how this would get me into trouble—if I didn't get married and become respectable. I think Frank must have put her up to it, you know, buying her a dress and getting her to influence me. I didn't want to get married. I was having such a good time. But Frank kept begging me and this woman kept on at me. So I married him so long as he never told my mother. He never did.' Indeed, Tillie

## Learning Young

Circa 1916.

West went to her grave without ever knowing that she once had a son-in-law.

Frank Wallace and Mae West were married on 11 April, 1911 in Milwaukee. He was twenty-one; she was eighteen. It remained a secret but not, as it turned out, forever.

# Mae West

Not surprisingly, the marriage (or what passed for it) was a disaster. From the outset Mae deeply regretted what she had done and felt dreadful about the deception she would have to sustain for the sake of her mother. Her treatment of Frank became intolerably cruel, and she continued to date other men indiscriminately. She behaved as if she was blotting out all vestiges of married life by behaving like a loose, single woman.

The marriage lasted no more than a few weeks, effectively, but not legally, ending when the tour did. Mae also truncated their professional partnership by dispatching Frank solo on another lengthy tour as a male hoofer. As she herself put it in her autobiography: 'He went out of my life except for a legal echo years later when I was a Hollywood motion picture star. I had made a mistake in marriage. I promised not to make it again. This one weird experience with matrimony made me respect the institution.'

If 1911 was the year in which Mae West married and separated, it was also the year in which she finally made it to Broadway. Her one-time teacher Ned Wayburn effected an introduction between Mae and Jesse L. Lasky. Lasky, an erstwhile cornet player and vaudevillian, was soon to become one of the lynchpins of Paramount Pictures. In 1911, however, he owned The Folies Bergère, a theatre-cum-restaurant in the heart of Broadway, and was looking for an ingénue to take part in a show called *A La Broadway*. Mae fitted the bill and found herself working with a comedy duo called Cook and Lorenz for whom she was required to play a maid and sing a couple of songs. The words for the songs were provided by a young lyricist who, in the thirties, became an important producer in Hollywood: William Le Baron.

## Learning Young

Unhappy with some of Le Baron's lyrics, Mae took it upon herself to work them over to suit her particular personality. On the opening night of the show in the presence of Florenz Ziegfeld, the powerful Shubert brothers, and her parents, she made quite an impact, taking encore after encore. The influential *New York Times* referred to Mae as a 'hitherto unknown (who) pleased by her grotesquerie and a snappy way of singing and dancing,' while the *Tribune* commented on her 'sense of nonsense, which is the very latest addition to wit.' The *Herald* let its readers know that she 'danced in Turkish harem trousers in a most amusing, energetic, and carefree manner,' while the *Evening World* noted that 'it was on Miss Mae West's appearance that the first real hit was made. She seems to be a sort of female George M. Cohan with an amusing, impudent manner.'

Her 'amusing, impudent manner' which would soon become so indelibly linked with the mature West persona was not, however, enough to save Lasky's nightclub. The Folies closed after only eight performances, at a loss of over $100,000—a considerable amount of money in 1911.

Once again Mae West was unemployed. But not, however, unemployable. Lee Shubert, who was at the opening of *A La Broadway*, was sufficiently impressed by the newcomer to offer her a small part in the Shubert brothers' new show, *Vera Violetta*, starring the great Al Jolson. This lavish extravaganza was designed to compete with Ziegfeld's popular *Follies* and had songs by Edward Eysler. It opened without Mae West. Prior to the official first night on 11 November, 1911, Mae went down with a heavy cold and missed the first six performances, including the all-

Mae West

Mae West used this saucy 1918 song in her vaudeville act. From the collections of Roy Bishop and Harold Jacobs.

important press night. She returned to the show the following week and stayed with it for the remainder of the run.

# Learning Young

Ziegfeld himself beckoned next, and on 12 April, 1912, Mae opened in *A Winsome Widow,* playing a character called La Petite Daffs. She was by no means the star of the show (comedian Frank Tinney and The Dolly Sisters were) and although she did have a song to sing (called 'Piccolo'), the trade paper *Variety* gave Mae her first bad review. Its dyspeptic reviewer wrote that a 'pretty melody [had been] spoiled in the singing by Mae West, a rough soubrette...just a bit too coarse.' This may have been the first, but was by no means the last time the adjective 'coarse' would be applied to her.

Mae remained with *A Winsome Widow* for 172 performances. She then teamed up with Harry Laughlin and Bobby O'Neill, two dancers from *A La Broadway* whose names, she suggested, be changed to The Girard Brothers. Their act was called Mae West and the Girard Brothers.

In 1913 she appeared in variety at the Fifth Avenue Theatre. She even, for a while, became part of an act with her sister Beverly. The result gave the popular Dolly Sisters no cause for concern whatsoever. Beverly's intrinsic lack of talent and the differences in temperament between the sisters made working together impossible. Even with Mae in charge, Beverley wasn't much; without her, she was nothing and, sadly, she knew it. Their act was called Sisters, and it drew from *Variety*'s reviewer the ho-hum observation that 'it isn't quite as rough as Mae West can't help being,' followed by '...unless Mae West can tone down her stage presence in every way she might just as well hop out of vaudeville into burlesque.' Though the brunt of the criticism was leveled at Mae, it was, ironically, Beverly who took to drink.

# Mae West

In 1916, when Mae was twenty-three, she met James A. Timony. He was extremely personable, dashing, well-built thirty-eight-year-old who owned a baseball team and had amassed a great deal of money out of racing cars and planes. He was of Irish-Catholic descent, and, after being introduced to Mae by Tillie—who thought a man of his wealth and connections could be of use to her daughter—he fell in love with her. He remained in love with her for the rest of his life.

Though Mae's feelings for Jim Timony in no way matched his, they nevertheless became lovers—a fact that did not prevent Mae from having other affairs whenever the opportunity arose. Jim also became her manager—and the one man in her life she could trust implicitly.

In her next professional engagement, she teamed up with singer-pianist Harry Richman who, in 1930, starred in the early Hollywood musical *Puttin' on the Ritz* with a score by Irving Berlin. In 1916, though, he was still a struggling performer waiting for his big break. He did not get it with Mae. She dominated the partnership and her incipient vulgarity hardly allowed him a look-in. According to Richman, West would not take a cent less than a pricey $500 per week for the act ($300 for her, $200 for him). As a result of this, their bookings dwindled and the act finally dissolved.

Nothing, however, could dissolve Mae's determination to become as big a star as her more famous contemporaries—Jolson, Sophie Tucker, Eddie Cantor, Gaby Deslys, Will Rogers, Eva Tanguay, and Fanny Brice—all of whom were earning big money topping bills for the likes of Ziegfeld, Klaw and Erlanger, and Edward F. Albee of the powerful Keith circuit. She wasn't in their league yet—as

## Learning Young

the reviewers were not shy to confirm—but she was learning all the time and continued to hone her natural abilities in theaters across the country.

It was in Chicago that Mae discovered jazz. Shortly after America entered World War I in April 1917 the country, in a spirit of frenzy, went dance mad. Visiting a 'colored' night club called The Elite on the city's South Side, she was overwhelmed by the excitement and the sexiness of the routines as performed by the club's sinewy black dancers. The next day, during a matinee at the Majestic Theatre, she decided to incorporate some of those steps into her act and uninhibitedly shimmied and shook to roars of approval. Though the management protested, anticipating riots and police raids (neither of which were forthcoming), Mae continued to pepper her act with her new, Negro-inspired steps. The following year she introduced them to Broadway in Arthur Hammerstein's production of Rudolf Friml's musical *Sometime*.

Though once again Mae was not the star—Ed Wynn and Francine Larrimore were—she received Hammerstein's approval to pad out her supporting role of Mame Dean with her shimmy in a song called 'Any Kind Of Man.' Yet again *Variety* dissented: 'Miss West,' its reviewer noted, 'has improved somewhat in looks, but is still the rough hand-on-hip character that she first conceived.' Quite clearly, the West persona was, by 1918, just waiting to be hatched. But the time wasn't right. Either Mae wasn't ready for Broadway, or Broadway wasn't ready for Mae.

*Sometime* closed after a run of 283 performances—which, given the buoyant climate of Broadway in the late teens and the sheer volume of new shows that opened each

Mae West

A 1923 sheet music cover. From the collections of Roy Bishop and Harold Jacobs.

## Learning Young

week—wasn't at all bad. Indeed, no musical that season ran longer. But instead of staying on and touring with the show, Mae once again decided to go it alone. She drew inspiration, this time, not from Black jazz clubs, but from the unique Texas ('Hello, suckers') Guinan, whose New York niterie was a famous watering hole for the city's underworld. Mae West and Texas Guinan were not unalike in their unabashed vulgarity, and, though Mae never said as much—and even denied it to me when I put it to her—the image she was to project to the world fifteen years later owed much to 'the queen of the speakeasies.'

Between 1919 and 1921 Mae continued to earn a living in vaudeville and revue and was invited by J. J. Shubert to appear in a show he was directing called *The Mimic World* at the New Century. It flopped dismally, but during its short run Mae did get to meet a man she worshipped. He was heavyweight champion Jack Dempsey who had recently made boxing history by beating Georges Carpentier in the sport's first million-dollar match. After the opening night of *The Mimic World* on 15 August, 1921, Dempsey's manager, Jack Kearns, brought the prizefighter backstage, hoping the two would hit it off and—the real purpose of the introduction—possibly make a movie together. The film Kearns had in mind was an adventure called *Daredevil Jack*, but Jim Timony, jealous of his client-cum-lover's obvious attraction to Dempsey, vetoed the idea on the grounds that she couldn't synchronize movie making with her heavy touring schedule. As Mae had come to rely more and more on Timony's judgment, she reluctantly accepted the decision and for the next four years continued peddling her act across the country. Then, in 1925, and with star status having still eluded her, she made a decision that would change her life.

Mae West

From the collections of Roy Bishop and Harold Jacobs.

# Chapter 3

# MAE the PLAYWRIGHT

In 1925, at the age of thirty-two, Mae West realized that the reason she had never really made it on Broadway in a 'book' show was that her personality was too clearly defined to be shoe-horned into roles that were not written specifically for her. As far back as 1911, she had rewritten William Le Baron's lyrics for *A La Broadway* to bring them more into line with her particular style and delivery. It now struck her that if she wanted to make any kind of impact on the highly competitive New York stage, she'd have to write a play with a bespoke part in it for herself. The result was a 'sex drama' called *The Albatross*. Its central character was Margie LaMont, a prostitute who, after saving a society hostess from a drug overdose, is charged with theft by the very woman whose life she saved. In retaliation, Margie snares the woman's son into marriage, but at the last minute reconsiders her actions before ditching the boy for the young sailor she has always loved.

# Mae West

As Mae herself put it, 'I didn't bother with any approach. I just sat down and wrote the kind of show I'd like to see myself.'

Uncharacteristically, she did not yet have the confidence to attach her own name to the play, and it opened as the work of 'Jane Mast.' It had been rejected outright by the Shuberts, but Jim Timony decided to finance it himself. The well-known English-born racketeer Owney Madden—a good friend of Mae's—also put money into the production; so did C. William Morgenstern, who was given the producer's credit. The director they chose was Edward Eisner, whose track record had included working with John Barrymore, Gaby Deslys, and Maud Adams. After a chaotic rehearsal period followed by a troubled out-of-town run at the New London Theatre in Connecticut, the show's title was changed from *The Albatross* to the less equivocal *Sex*.

To generate publicity for the New York opening, Mae erroneously put it about that several newspapers refused to print the play's title in the ads. It finally opened at Daly's Theatre in New York on 26 April, 1926. 'Nasty, infantile, amateurish,' pronounced *Variety*. 'Stark naked lust' said the *Herald Tribune*, whose reviewer concluded 'Miss Mae West added but little to the art of entertainment.'

Though *Sex* opened to modest box office returns, it soon began to find its audience. The play's come-hither title was constantly the butt of outraged editorials—especially from the *New York Daily Mirror* and *The Graphic*—and generated enough publicity to keep it in the public eye. So did a plagiarism suit which lasted six months before it was thrown out of court. In the end, and regardless of the poor notices, *Sex* ran for over a year.

## Mae the Playwright

Mae's next excursion into playwriting dealt with male homosexuality. Despite her own healthy sexual appetite and her penchant for 'real men,' she enjoyed the company of homosexuals, and the feeling was mutual. They were no threat to her, and she, with her camp, over-the-top, almost caricatural approach to sex, was certainly no threat to them.

The new play, ahead of its time in preaching tolerance for homosexuals, was called *The Drag* and was especially sympathetic towards transvestites. At the same time, Mae was not unaware of the inflammatory, taboo nature of the subject, nor of the publicity it would most surely generate. Once again she used her pseudonym, Jane Mast, and again Eisner and Morgenstern served as director and producer. This time, though, Mae chose not to appear in it. It would have been most unwise for someone who herself could so easily have passed as a female impersonator (and whom some people to this day believe *was* a man in drag!) to compete with real transvestites. Audiences would be confused and the whole point of the play lost.

The first performance of *The Drag* took place at Poli's Park Theatre in Bridgeport, Connecticut in January, 1927. Despite another pan in *Variety* ('a cheap and shabby appeal to sensationalism...without intelligence or taste') the show did well enough at the box office to move to Paterson, New Jersey for another short engagement, and thence to New Jersey's Opera House in Bayonne. There, on 10 February, the local chief of police announced to the packed opening night audience that the play was being banned and that their money would be refunded.

A New York run was planned, but that, too, was not to happen, for the night before the anticipated Bayonne

# Mae West

premiere of *The Drag,* Daly's Theatre in New York, where Mae and *Sex* were still appearing, was raided. So were two other theatres: The Empire which housed a play about lesbianism called *The Captive,* and The Princess whose offending offering was *The Virgin Man.*

On 19 April, 1927 Mae, together with her mother Tillie and her sister Beverly (who had understudied for Mae) as well as nineteen other members of the cast of *Sex,* appeared in court. The prosecutor's case was that the play's central character, Margie LaMont, glorified prostitution. Enjoying the sheer absurdity of it all, Mae gave new meaning to the term *show trial* by turning the hearing into a farce. The packed court was delighted with her performance; ('The audience wants dirt and I give it to them,' she said). The jury was not however and, after considering their verdict, found Mae, Jim Timony, and producer Morgenstern guilty of corrupting the morals of youth. Each was fined $500 and sentenced to prison for ten days.

Though Mae's incarceration at Welfare Island brought her into contact with the city's flotsam and jetsam, she made the best of it, absorbed 'local color,' had two days knocked off her sentence for good behavior, and, if her own account of her confinement is to be believed, found herself enjoying the company of the prison's warden, who called her 'a fine woman'!

Notwithstanding all the publicity attracted by her trial and imprisonment, Timony thought it prudent to close *Sex* and to abandon all thoughts of bringing *The Drag* into New York. Mae, who did not fancy a second term at Welfare Island, agreed.

Her next play, she decided, would be less controversial. *The Wicked Age,* again directed by Eisner, was an exposé of the

## Mae the Playwright

Mae put on a brave face about her run-in with the law and time in jail, extracting full publicity value.

world of rigged bathing beauty contests and featured Wilva Davis and a woefully miscast movie actor called Raymond Jarno. It was a disaster and closed after just four weeks.

# Mae West

Outside the Grand Jury room.

And then, at long last, it happened: the big break Mae had been waiting for all her life. It came about, or so she claimed in her autobiography, as a result of a conversation she had with a hotel porter. Mae, who was dressed to kill in

## Mae the Playwright

her jewels and finery, reminded the porter of a woman he once knew at the turn of the century. She came from the Bowery, he said, and launched into a colorful description of the place as it had been twenty-five years earlier, with its gang warfare, brothels, and saloons.

The description immediately fired Mae's imagination. If the Bowery during 'the gay nineties' was the perfect setting for a 'sex drama,' the character she reminded the hotel porter of was just the sort of creation Mae knew she could bring vividly to life. She'd call her Diamond Lil. As for the plot, it would be about a saloon singer who falls in love with a Salvation Army officer, unaware that he is really a detective in disguise. White slavery would feature prominently in it—so, too, Mae decided, would her sister Beverly, playing an innocent who attempts suicide and falls into the hands of white slavers after being abandoned by the man she loves. It was a heady concoction to be sure, meaty as well as romantic, and she found no difficulty in persuading a willing Owney Madden to become one of the show's more heavily committed 'angels.' The director was Ira Hards.

On 11 April, 1928, *Diamond Lil* opened at the Royale Theatre on Broadway, competing that record-breaking season with such shows as Elmer Rice's *Street Scene*, Ben Hecht and Charles MacArthur's *The Front Page*, Kern and Hammerstein's *Showboat*, and George S. Kaufman and Edna Ferber's *The Royal Family*, inspired by the Barrymore clan.

*Diamond Lil* was a smash-hit and ran until 12 January the following year. Suddenly Mae West was up there with Lynn Fontanne, Helen Hayes, Jane Cowl, and Ina Claire as Broadway's newest sweetheart. 'Pure trash, or impure trash...I wouldn't miss *Diamond Lil* if I were you' said the

# Mae West

*Diamond Lil,* 1928, finally brought Mae the praises of the top critics and a financial hit as well.

hard-to-please *New Yorker,* while the *Evening Telegram* generously referred to Mae as 'so regal...so assured...so devastating...so blonde...so buxom...so beautiful...that she makes Miss Ethel Barrymore look like the late lamented Bert Savoy. From now on she's my favorite actress. She's simply superb.' The intellectual *New Republic* was equally enthusiastic. 'She is alive on stage as nobody is in life,' wrote its critic, while even the staid *New York Times* conceded she was 'a good actress.'

Mae West had finally made it in a role (and a period) that would forever be associated with her. At the age of thirty-five she had become a star and Broadway was at her feet.

## Mae the Playwright

Mae also sang 'Easy Rider' in *She Done Him Wrong*, the film version of *Diamond Lil*. From the collections of Roy Bishop and Harold Jacobs.

# Mae West

Forever fearless and now emboldened by the success of *Diamond Lil*, Mae's next play, which she called *Pleasure Man* (and in which she did not appear) tackled the subjects of adultery, transvestism (borrowed from *The Drag*) and castration. It was the story of an actor whose lover, a married woman, discovers that he has been murdered by castration. The culprit turns out to be the brother of a young girl with whose affections the promiscuous actor once dallied.

Openly controversial, provocative, and ahead of its time (Tennessee Williams was to use the castration theme in his 1959 success *Sweet Bird Of Youth*), the play, which opened at the Biltmore Theatre on 6 October, 1929, lost Mae all the kudos she had won earlier in the year. 'Such filth as turns one's stomach' wrote the *Evening Post*, while the *Sun*'s reviewer, the respected Gilbert W. Gabriel, referred to its 'sickening excess of filth.' As had happened with her play *Sex*, the New York police, their Black Marias to the ready, hauled everyone concerned with the production to the West 47th Street precinct. The charge, inevitably, was indecency. Jim Timony managed to obtain a court injunction that temporarily prevented further police intervention and allowed the play to continue the following evening. The District Attorney, however, taking the advice of the public prosecutor, invalidated the injunction and arrested the cast after the third performance. Mae declared her willingness to stand trial once again, and even hired a powerful lawyer, Nathan Burkan, to defend her. The trial date was set for 14 March, 1930. It resulted in a hung jury after which the assistant district attorney, James Garrett Wallace, let it be known he would not be seeking a retrial. Mae had won on points.

## Mae the Playwright

All the same, *Pleasure Man* ran for only two troubled performances before becoming just one more Broadway casualty. *Diamond Lil*, on the other hand, still had 'legs' and, after it closed in New York, Mae took it to Chicago, San Francisco, and Los Angeles. It returned in triumph for a New York re-play, its success marred only by the impending *Pleasure Man* trial and by Tillie's death, at the age of fifty-six, from a cancerous liver. Although comforted by Battling Jack, her sister Beverly, and her brother John (who had always been closer to their flamboyant father), and by the faithful and reliable Jim Timony, Mae was inconsolable.

She went into a deep decline, claimed she no longer wanted to live, and temporarily allowed her grief to affect her mental state. In Mae's mind there was no one who could take the place of her beloved mother, and she lost a dramatic thirty pounds in weight. Fortunately, she still had *Diamond Lil* to keep her occupied at night and was spared the added calamity of the Wall Street collapse, most of her accumulated wealth being invested in jewelry rather than stock.

As Mae slowly came to grips with the reality of her mother's passing, she decided to write a novel. Initially called *Babe Gordon*, but later changed to *The Constant Sinner*, it was the steamy saga of Babe, a Harlem prostitute who becomes the mistress of a rich playboy. Murder, suicide, auto-eroticism, homosexuality, an inter-racial affair and the low-life world of drug peddlers and racketeers were appliquéd onto the central narrative line. It was published, after a great deal of editing and rewriting, by The Macaulay Co. and became a controversial bestseller. So much so that impresario J. J. Shubert persuaded Mae to adapt it as a play.

# Mae West

He needn't have bothered. The result—an out-and-out melodrama in twenty-one scenes, requiring a cast of over fifty actors—opened at the Royale on 13 September, 1931 to reviews that ranged from indifferent to downright hostile. It was clearly not what Depression-weary audiences wanted to see, and it closed after eight weeks, plunging Mae into one of the lowest spots of her life. The success of *Diamond Lil* began to look like nothing more than a mirage. After six years as a practicing Broadway playwright, and just one year before she turned forty, her career seemed over.

She had not, however, reckoned on Hollywood.

# Chapter 4

# HOORAY for HOLLYWOOD

It was no secret that the advent of the radio, and, later, the growing popularity of the movies, were responsible for the death of vaudeville. With the arrival, in 1927, of what was initially called the 'talkers,' Hollywood, the film capital of the world, had overnight become an open door for some of the best talent Broadway could offer—as well as a graveyard for several prominent silent screen stars whose voices were unsuitable for sound pictures. Also, with the coming of sound, a new genre of film had burst onto a willing world: the screen musical. Naturally, before the invention of the talkies (as they eventually came to be known) there was little call for the musical talents of stars like Al Jolson, Marilyn Miller, George M. Cohan, Helen Morgan, Eddie Cantor, The Marx Brothers and Fanny Brice. But that all changed on 6 October, 1927, after the ground-breaking premiere of Warner Bros. *The Jazz Singer* in which Jolson sang several songs and uttered

# Mae West

With George Raft in *Night after Night*, 1932.

the first words ever spoken in a feature film. The floodgates were open.

Two of the people Mae had worked with in 1911, Jesse Lasky and William Le Baron, had, in the 1920s, decided to abandon Broadway for Hollywood where they both did pretty well for themselves. Lasky became second in command to Adolph Zukor at Paramount Pictures, while Le Baron turned his talents from lyric writing to production,

## Hooray for Hollywood

first at United Artists, then at Paramount. In 1929, after disagreements with both Zukor and Lasky, Le Baron defected to RKO studios, where he produced the successful musical *Rio Rita* with John Boles and Bebe Daniels. Lured by financial inducements however, he returned to Paramount in 1932 and began work with a relative newcomer to Hollywood, George Raft.

During the run of Mae's play *Sex*, Raft, who was then known as Rauft, worked for racketeer Owney Madden, delivering bootleg liquor for him. He and Mae met, were instantly attracted to each other, and had a brief but passionate affair after which their lives took separate routes. Rauft fetched up in Hollywood, changed his surname to Raft and, with his exotic Latin looks, entered pictures in 1929 with *Queen of the Nightclubs*. Three years later he scored his first big success as the coin-flipping Capone-like gangster in Howard Hawks' *Scarface*.

It was Raft who was responsible for Mae West's Hollywood career—and Mae acknowledged this to Lewis Yablonsky, Raft's biographer. The film in question was *Night After Night* (1932), directed by Archie Mayo, in which Raft starred (opposite Constance Cummings and Alison Skipworth) as an ex-prizefighter who runs a swanky nightclub. There was a role in it that had still to be cast—the character of Maudie Triplett, one of Raft's past flames. Le Baron initially wanted Texas Guinan, but the 'queen of the speakeasies' was looking rather too lived-in for the close scrutiny of the cameras. It was then that Raft, probably by association, remembered Mae West. So did Le Baron. Though the general feeling amid the Paramount hierarchy was that Mae was a bit of a has-been, a Broadway

45

# Mae West

joke, her curiosity value couldn't harm the picture. After all, Mae West *had* made a name for herself, even if it was only on the East coast. Besides, as it was a supporting role, what could they lose? They signed her for two months at a generous $5,000 a week.

Mae left New York by train in June, 1932 and arrived in Pasadena, California accompanied by Jim Timony and her sister Beverly. The studio had arranged accommodations at the Ravenswood Apartments on fashionable Rossmore Avenue. Mae did not initially take to the film capital of the world. And, it must be said, the feeling was mutual. Having enjoyed the fruits of stardom in New York, she knew that in Hollywood she was nothing and nobody. She also knew that the role she had been signed for wasn't large and that, on her first day at the studio, she would not be sailing through the famous Paramount gates as a star.

Mae had what in contemporary parlance one might describe as an 'attitude' problem. When the script for *Night After Night* was sent to her, she let her dissatisfaction with the screenplay in general and her part in it in particular be known. 'I didn't like it,' she informed the *Sunday Dispatch* in London, 'and I told them so in several different languages.' Not only that, but she flatly refused to begin filming unless she was allowed to rewrite her own material just as she had done with Le Baron on *A La Broadway* twenty-one years before. She even offered to return the weekly pay check she'd been receiving if they said no. But fortunately for the future history of Hollywood, Adolph Zukor reluctantly agreed to let her wield her pen. From then on she spent a great deal of time on the set trying to get the 'feel' of motion pictures and reassessing her approach to comedy. For Mae

# Mae West

Mae never smoked, but posed with Hollywood's requisite vamp accessory for her first film, *Night After Night*, 1932.

was shrewd enough to realize that what worked on stage in front of a live audience didn't necessarily work in front of a camera. As she told me herself when I interviewed her, unlike Broadway, where she traded in body language rather than one-liners, in the movies she had to come up with wisecracks to compensate for the physical things the censors would not allow her to do—like sitting on a man's lap. 'And, honey, I've been on more laps than a napkin.'

The impact Mae made in what was an otherwise indifferent movie, was tremendous. 'Goodness, what lovely diamonds,' exclaims a hat-check girl when Mae, outfitted in furs and jewels, first walks into Raft's nightclub. 'Goodness had nothing to do with it, dearie.' replies Mae, hand on hip and looking, as some wag once described her, 'like an upholstered egg-cup.' It was a line that immediately zinged its way into Hollywood legend. What Mae never acknowledged, though, was that it originated with Texas Guinan.

True authorship notwithstanding, the gag and its unique delivery went some considerable distance to launching Mae West into Hollywood stardom. So enormous was her impact in *Night After Night* that cinema managers across America pestered Paramount to feature her in a film of her own.

At the time Paramount was going through a bad patch financially, and the acute Zukor realized that part of the solution to filling the studio's diminishing coffers could be Mae West. She had the shrewd idea of turning her greatest creation and biggest success, *Diamond Lil*, into her first starring vehicle. It was, she persuaded Zukor, the obvious choice.

# Mae West

Cary Grant with Mae in *She Done Him Wrong*, 1933.

With script approval, a different director (Lowell Sherman), and a personable leading man called Cary Grant, whom Mae claimed to have 'discovered' on the studio lot, shooting commenced on the movie that would make stars of both its leading players. Grant was cast as the mission man Mae takes a shine to, and their on-screen chemistry was electric.

Needless to say, the script came in for criticism. It had been sanitized by scenarists Harvey Thew and John Bright to meet the demands of the Hays Office, formed in 1930, but the vigilant president, Will H. Hays, still demanded that the

## Hooray for Hollywood

Cheesecake photos were required of most new Hollywood actresses, unless they were noted Shakespearean exponents.

central character's overt bawdiness be watered down, even insisting on a change of title. Mae disapproved. But she was dealing with an organization far more powerful than she was and had no choice but to comply. The title she

# Mae West

More cheesecake, Victorian style.

eventually settled for was *She Done Him Wrong* and the central character was renamed Lady Lou. She compensated for the further cuts the Hays Office demanded by peppering the script with wisecracks. 'When women go wrong, men go right after them,' says Lou, consoling a distraught innocent who has strayed. 'It takes two to get one in trouble.' 'Diamonds is my career,' and 'It was a toss-up whether I go in for diamonds or sing in the choir. The choir lost.'

# Hooray for Hollywood

The film, of course, is also famous for introducing her well-known catchphrase. It is universally misquoted as 'Come up and see me sometime,' but actually runs 'Why don't you come up sometime and see me?'

*She Done Him Wrong* (1933), which also starred Gilbert Roland, was shot, in sequence, in eighteen days, three days ahead of schedule, and at a cost of $200,000. Despite the censorship strictures it remains one of Mae West's most outspoken 'sex dramas'—and one of her funniest. She looks radiant throughout, and Sherman's direction maintains just the right pace.

It is interesting to note that the sexy walk Mae had developed for herself came about as a result of the shoes she asked Paramount's head of costume, Travis Banton, to

Paramount publicity photo, 1933.

## Mae West

From the collections of Roy Bishop and Harold Jacobs.

## Hooray for Hollywood

design for her. Being physically small, she wanted extra height, and Banton obliged by giving her six-inch heels which he artfully covered by the full-length gowns he designed for her. Wearing six-inch heels, however, was no easy accomplishment, and the so-called sexy walk Mae adopted had less to do with sex than with her way of coping with discomfort. That it looked sexy was an added bonus.

The movie grossed an impressive $3 million for the studio and turned Mae into a household name on a par with such major Paramount stars of the time as Clara Bow, Claudette Colbert, Miriam Hopkins, Herbert Marshall, Maurice Chevalier, Gary Cooper, The Marx Brothers, Carole Lombard and Marlene Dietrich. (Dietrich, like Mae, was married to a man—Rudolph Sieber—she hardly saw and never lived with.)

Mae West became a sensation, not only in America, but throughout Europe. From one Paris correspondent came this extravagant eulogy: 'She has been compared to Réjane in *ZaZa*...she was discovered by *littérateurs* as the perfect illustration of the early works of De Maupassant...and playwrights hailed her as possessing the dialoguing genius of the Commedia dell'arte.'

Despite its many happy box office returns, *She Done Him Wrong* was banned in Australia and offended several religious groups which found the West persona objectionable. While the movie was still enjoying its initial run, a Catholic Bishop called Bernard Sheil formed a body known as the Legion of Decency whose avowed mission was to sanitize the morals of Hollywood and the movies it made.

## Mae West

*She Done Him Wrong*, 1933, film version of *Diamond Lil*.

Concerned but undaunted by the outraged criticisms being hurled from some quarters at his newest star, Zukor, was keen to have Mae follow up *She Done Him Wrong* with another starring vehicle as soon as possible. The subject she chose was based on a story by Lowell Brentano revolving

# Hooray for Hollywood

*I'm No Angel*, 1933.

around a lady lion tamer called Tira. Mae was fascinated by lions and saw potential in the property, which she provocatively titled *I'm No Angel*. Though the screenplay was structured by Brentano and Harlan Thompson, Mae, as usual, wrote all her own dialogue. She engaged Wesley Ruggles to direct her through the story of a carnival entertainer, Tira, who climbing the social ladder 'wrong by wrong,' sets her sights on a wealthy socialite, hoping in the process to raise her own social status. When he refuses to marry her, she slaps a million-dollar breach of promise suit on him. In the end, as always, Mae gets her man. The producer was William Le Baron. As Mae herself described it: 'It's all about a girl who lost her reputation, but never missed it.'

# Mae West

Cary Grant was again Mae's leading man in *I'm No Angel*, 1933.

Once again the new star chose Gary Grant as the object of her affection, and, although Grant does not appear in the movie until about halfway through, their sexual chemistry is terrific. It is never more so than in the scene in which Mae, seated at the piano to sing 'I Want You, I Need You,' gives him one of the most suggestive looks ever committed to celluloid, and then, rolling her eyes in a swooning gesture, kisses him. The rest of the cast included Gregory Ratoff and Gertrude Michael, and, as Beulah, who was so memorably summoned to 'peel me a grape,' Gertrude Howard.

## Hooray for Hollywood

As Tira in *I'm No Angel*, 1933.

## Mae West

*I'm No Angel* opened on 4 October, 1933. A week later Mordaunt Hall in the *New York Times* hailed it as a 'rapid-fire entertainment with shameless but thoroughly contagious humor...[Mae West] is a remarkable wit—after her fashion.' It was an even greater success than *She Done Him Wrong*, and, despite the disapproval it predictably generated among the morally outraged, played to packed houses wherever it was shown.

Indeed, the film was a triumph—the peak of Mae West's extraordinary, volatile career. Certainly she never made a better—or wittier—movie. 'I see a new position for you,' an astrologer tells Tira. 'Sitting or reclining?' she asks. 'When may I see you—breakfast, lunch, dinner?' asks Grant. 'Well I always have breakfast in bed—so that's out,' comes the reply. 'One figure can always add up to a lot...' Tira purrs seductively; and when Gertrude Michael tells her, 'You haven't a streak of decency in you,' Tira ripostes: 'I don't show my good points to strangers.' The movie also gave birth to the line: 'I've been things and seen places.'

In 1934, Mae, whose annual income had risen to an awesome $340,000, was at the top of the heap, and, more importantly for her personal esteem, being taken seriously by writers such as F. Scott Fitzgerald, who wrote of her: 'In a world of Garbos, Barrymores, Harlows, Valentinos, and Clara Bows, Mae West is the only type with an ironic edge, a comic spark, that takes on a more cosmopolitan case of life's enjoyments.' And writer Hugh Walpole noted 'Only Charlie Chaplin and Mae West in Hollywood dare directly attack with their mockery the fraying morals and manners of a dreary world.'

# Hooray for Hollywood

French poster for *I'm No Angel*.

All the same, despite her celebrity she wasn't accepted by filmdom's blue-bloods, being regarded, despite the Cadillacs she drove and the diamonds she sported (or, perhaps because of them), as intrinsically vulgar. This rejection must have irked her. Nonetheless, in her unreliable, often fictitious autobiography, *Goodness Had Nothing to Do with It*, she wrote of this particular period in her career: 'My personal life kept pace with my public one. I played as hard as I worked, did not neglect my pleasures, but I did wish I had more time for them.'

Because of movies like *She Done Him Wrong* and *I'm No Angel*—and the terrific controversy they attracted—the powerful Legion of Decency made quite sure that by 1934 screen censorship would be stricter than ever before in Hollywood's hitherto permissive history. The Hays Office,

# Mae West

Roger Pryor is one of Mae's suitors in *Belle of the Nineties*, 1934.

now under a Catholic journalist called Joseph Breen, devised a brand new Production Code of do's and don'ts that would, for the next twenty years or so, put a stranglehold on what the movies could say or show. It was, for example, a Production Code stricture that forbade a man and a woman to share a double bed, even if they were married. And if a man kissed his wife while on a bed, he had to make sure that one foot was resting squarely on the floor.

It was in this sensitive moral climate that Mae began to put together her next film, tentatively called *That St. Louis Woman*, later altered to *It Ain't No Sin*, under which title Paramount's publicity department set about planning its ad campaign. Naturally, the latter title was unacceptable to the

# Hooray for Hollywood

Johnny Mack Brown is among Pryor's rivals who also include arch villain John Miljan. *Belle of the Nineties* was directed by Leo McCarey.

# Mae West

*Belle of the Nineties*, 1934. Costume designer Travis Banton outdid himself.

# Hooray for Hollywood

Edith Head, later a noted designer, worked as Travis Banton's assistant when he did this Statue of Liberty gown for *Belle of the Nineties*. Head did an homage to this costume when she designed Mae's gowns for *Myra Breckenridge* in 1970.

# Mae West

Breen Office because of its religious connotations, and its name was once again changed, this time to the innocuous *Belle of the Nineties*. It was endemic of the trouble Mae was to have with the screenplay she wrote for it, a trifle involving the rivalry between a pair of suitors for the affections of Ruby Carter, the star of New Orleans' Sensation House. ('I prefer two kinds of men: domestic and foreign.') Mae, of course, was Ruby, a lady very much in the Tira mould, and although the censor imposed his sanctimonious will on the script, there was no way he was able to change Mae's libidinous personality or the walk that launched a thousand female impersonator's hips. Mae was once again a smash, and although her budget was four times the amount of her previous efforts (about $800,000), *Belle of the Nineties*, released in September 1934, immediately went into profit on its release and grossed in excess of $2 million.

Roger Pryor co-starred as Tiger Kid, the good man she falls for; while John Miljan was the villain of the piece. ('His mother should have thrown him away and kept the stork.') Duke Ellington and His Band, no less, accompanied Mae in the musical numbers, the majority of which were composed by Arthur Johnston and Sam Coslow. Leo McCarey, who had recently had a hit with the Marx Brothers on *Duck Soup*, directed, and the producer once again was William Le Baron.

Physically, it was the lushest, best-looking movie Mae had made to date—or would ever make. She looked stunning in it, regardless of the fact that, due to irreversible problems she was having with her hair at the time, she wore a wig throughout. And, of course, the usual oneliners were there in abundance. As Ruby walks through a hotel lobby, the manager points to an oil painting of a

# Hooray for Hollywood

*Every Day's a Holiday*, 1937.

# Mae West

*Belle of the Nineties,* 1934.

woman. 'This one is an old master,' he tells her. 'Looks more like an old mistress to me,' comes the retort. And when someone remarks to Ruby that all she thinks about is having a good time, Ruby replies 'I don't only think about it.'

# Hooray for Hollywood

'It's better to be looked over than over-looked' is another of Ruby's quips and, most typical of all, when in the midst of an embrace a suitor tells her 'I must have you. Your golden hair, your fascinating eyes, your alluring smile, your lovely arms, your form divine...' she asks, 'Is this a proposal or are you taking an inventory?'

The film was another smash for Paramount, despite the expected cries of outrage it attracted in some quarters. Financially Mae had never been better off in her life, and she bought a hacienda in the San Fernando Valley. Beverly shared Mae's Ravenswood apartment with her, while Jim Timony, still acting as her manager, had one of his own in the same building. As for Mae's young brother John, through his famous sister's help he was given a job as a carpenter on the Paramount lot, but an increasing fondness for alcohol made sure he didn't keep it. Which left Battling

# Mae West

Jack. Mae had bought her father an estate back east on Long Island, but several unwise real estate investments in Florida left him broke. Mae sent for him, and after his arrival in California, he lived a life of leisure courtesy of his famous daughter.

In all, 1934 was a great year for Mae. With three smash-hits in a row she had, single-handedly, saved Paramount from bankruptcy and was rewarded for her efforts by becoming one of the highest paid women in America. Like Garbo, she had become a legend in her lifetime.

But the party was nearly over and her luck was about to change. The following year, 1935, was not to be one she could look back on with any fondness.

## Chapter 5

# HANGING IN

On 6 July, 1935, at the age of seventy-one, Mae's father, Battling Jack West, succumbed to a heart attack. Adding to Mae's problems was the unexpected return into her life of her husband, Frank Wallace. Despite her numerous affairs, Mae had, since hitting the big time, always been scrupulous about avoiding scandal, and Frank's sudden intrusion was the very last thing she needed or wanted.

What had happened was that their marriage certificate had surfaced in Milwaukee (where they plighted their troths way back in 1911). In 1935 anything that concerned Mae West was news. The discovery that one of the world's most celebrated sex goddesses was actually *married* was particularly newsworthy and it attracted journalists from all over the country.

Frank—who had bigamously married a woman in 1916 and divorced her in 1935—was eventually traced to New

# Mae West

York where he was eking out a meager living as a dancer. When interviewed on the subject, he admitted that, yes, he had been married to Mae West. A lengthy and complicated series of court actions followed these revelations. In 1937 he demanded half of Mae's fortune (estimated at $3 million) under California's joint property agreement, but didn't get it. Three years later he filed a hefty damages suit claiming that Mae and Jim Timony had threatened to ruin his stage career if he ever revealed that he and Mae were legally married. The suit was dismissed. The following year he filed another suit in San Bernardino, California, on the grounds that Mae had committed adultery and demanded a separation payment of $1,000 per month. Mae, in turn, asked for a divorce which was finally granted in July 1942.

In the interim, Paramount had put their controversial, money-making star to work on *Goin' to Town*, a typically Westian concoction except that she appeared in modern dress. She was also a few pounds heavier now—the weight very much in evidence on those parts of her body once occupied by voluptuous curves. The story of a cattle queen called Cleo Borden who inherits an oilfield, *Goin' to Town*'s main narrative thrust concerned Cleo's attempts to crash high society and become part of the Newport aristocracy.

Although Mae fashioned a screenplay for herself (from a story by Marion Morgan and George B. Dowell) that had its usual quota of gags ('I've been doing a lot of thinking about you lately,' says one of Cleo's suitors. 'Hmm. You must be awful tired,' comes the reply) there is a conspicuous lack of fun about the proceedings. Mae's attack on the *haute monde* seems too heartfelt for genuine enjoyment and imparts to the movie a decided sense of

Hanging In

From the collections of Roy Bishop and Harold Jacobs.

## Mae West

unease. Its very best moment is when Cleo sings 'Softly Awakes My Heart' from Saint-Saens' opera *Samson and Delilah*. ('I have a lot of respect for that dame. There's one lady barber that made good.') Alexander Hall directed and William Le Baron produced. At this point in Mae's stratospheric career, studio head Emmanuel Cohen had created a special production unit on the lot for her and had upped her annual income to $480,000.

All the same, *Goin' to Town*, which went out of its way to toe the censorship line, was hardly vintage West. Released in 1935, it played a healthy five weeks at Manhattan's Paramount Theatre, but the critics were beginning to carp. 'No amount of epigrammatic hyping can offset the silly story,' beefed *Variety*; 'The great lady is revealing intimations of mortality,' said the *New York Times*, whose reviewer ended his notice with the observation that *'Goin' to Town* is the least successful of the Mae West pictures.'

Six months were to pass before the commencement of *Klondike Annie*. Though the storyline for the new picture was again supplied by Marion Morgan and George B. Dowell, it bore a striking likeness to a play Mae had been dickering with for several years and which she called *Frisco Kate*. The setting was Mae's favorite (and luckiest) period, the Gay Nineties.

*Klondike Annie* was the only Mae West film that took on religion. It also stretched her range as an actress, allowing us glimpses of a less sunny and breezy personality than audiences had come to expect. Yet despite the religious aspect, or perhaps because of it, Mae had to be especially vigilant where the censorial Breen Office was concerned. The result was a screenplay decidedly short on innuendo. ('I can

# Hanging In

With Victor McLaglen in *Klondike Annie*, 1936.

always tell a lady,' remarks co-star Victor McLaglen, to which comes the reply, 'Yeah? What do you tell 'em?') But Mae functioning at only 60 proof was better than nothing, and enough true West seeped through to keep her fans amused.

The story had potential too: it was about a Barbary Coast broad (called Frisco Doll) who, after murdering her

# Mae West

With Harold Huber, 'King of Chinatown,' in *Klondike Annie*, 1936. Huber: 'What is the matter, my Pearl of Pearls?' Mae: 'Your Pearl of Pearls has come unstrung.'

Chinese lover (Harold Huber), hops on a freighter, takes the place of a recently deceased Salvation Army sister, and gives a decided shot in the arm to the mission services at which she finds herself officiating. The musical highlight was Mae singing Gene Austin's 'Occidental Woman in an Oriental Mood for Love.' Raoul Walsh directed and, again, William Le Baron produced.

Paramount's head of production, Emmanuel Cohen, had meanwhile left the studio. He was replaced by Ernst Lubitsch, the German-born director known for his elegant, witty style, the famous 'Lubitsch touch.' Lubitsch and his 'touch,' however, cut no ice with Mae West, who had her own particular touch and wasn't about to change. She and the great director disliked each other from the outset (the fact that he was never without a cigar only aggravated matters as far as she was concerned), and something of the enmity between them seems to have found its way onto the set of *Klondike Annie* and into the movie itself. It was Mae's darkest, least joyous film.

Adding to her dissatisfaction with the new regime at Paramount was the fact that, despite the watered down screenplay, the film was condemned by the East Coast Preview Committee as 'replete with insinuations, a typical Mae West picture with the usual amount of risqué wisecracks and obvious sex appeal.' Mae simply could not win. Whatever she did or didn't do, she'd always be accused of peddling sex. The holier-than-thou Hearst press was particularly incensed at her 'blasphemous' approach to religion and lambasted her for daring to impersonate a nun. 'Is it not time Congress did something about Mae West?' their editorials thundered.

The Paramount publicity department may also have been to blame, with their ad campaign for the movie brazenly declaring that Frisco Doll 'made the Frozen North...Red Hot!' Just par for the Mae West course.

# Mae West

*Klondike Annie, 1936.*

# Hanging In

Despite the tameness of its content, *Klondike Annie* was banned in Nebraska and deemed objectionable by practicing Catholics. The general public, amused by all the adverse publicity, flocked to see it and helped notch up yet another success for its star.

The critics, however, were less enthusiastic. The film opened on 11 March, 1936 at the Paramount in New York and was severely knocked by the *New York Times*: 'There is no place anywhere for the stupid substitute that Miss West is now trying to pass as comedy,' its reviewer wrote; while the *Herald Tribune* called it 'vulgar without being funny and rowdy without being gay.'

With these rather sour notes ringing in her ears, Mae was convinced that she needed a change of studio. What with the arrival of Lubitsch, whom she grew to detest, and her general lack of respect for the executive hierarchy, 'Paramount didn't seem like home to me anymore' she wrote in her autobiography. She was convinced they would use her until the public no longer cared, then unceremoniously dump her. So, amidst much legal wrangling, all of it extremely acrimonious, Mae and Paramount negotiated a deal whereby she would work under contract for Emmanuel Cohen (whose own behavior towards the studio hadn't been particularly kosher either), but with Paramount continuing to release her films.

The first venture under this new arrangement was an adaptation of Lawrence Riley's stage success, *Personal Appearance*. It had been purchased by Paramount as a vehicle for actress Gladys George, who had starred in it on Broadway. When Mae let it be known that she wanted it, Paramount, much to Miss George's chagrin, turned the

# Mae West

property over to Emmanuel Cohen who produced it as a vehicle for Mae with Henry Hathaway directing.

As usual, the star worked on the screenplay herself, changing the title to *Go West, Young Man*. It had nothing to do with editor Horace Greeley's famous 19th century remark; nor was it the advice given by a theatrical agent to an up-and-coming young female impersonator. It was, in fact, about a famous movie star called Mavis Arden who, when we first meet her, is on a personal appearance tour promoting her latest film. Because she has signed a contract that forbids her to marry for five years, she is traveling with her press agent (Warren William) whose purpose is to prevent her from becoming romantically involved. But, of course, she does—with a young inventor (Randolph Scott) whom she meets in rural Pennsylvania when her car breaks down. Complications ensue, for the young inventor has a sweetheart of his own (Margaret Perry). But it all works out satisfactorily. At the final fade, Scott and Perry are back together, and Mae and William are romantically paired, as we always knew they would be.

Though it had its amusing moments and its usual quota of quips ('a thrill a day keeps the chill away') the majority of the critics carped. Comparing Mae unfavorably with Gladys George, they also objected to the general watering down of the original play. 'She (Mae) never makes the central character sufficiently credible to be laughed at,' said New York's *Herald Tribune*, while the *Post* was beginning to find its star's mannerisms 'tedious.' Without the innuendos and the general shock value of some of her earlier scripts, there was, indeed, something predictable and lackluster about the cleaned-up Mae West, and audiences were

# Hanging In

*Go West Young Man*, 1936.

# Mae West

With Herman Bing in *Every Day's a Holiday*, 1937.

disappointed. She was putting on far too much weight, an observation cruelly reinforced by the Hearst publication, the *Motion Picture Herald*, whose reviewer also had a go at her 'pitiful' singing.

The box office receipts for *Go West, Young Man*, released in 1936, were hardly disastrous, but they weren't great either. Mae let Cohen know that she would be pretty sensational playing Catherine the Great (a pet project of hers), but he felt that what the public really wanted from her were plots and characters rooted in the Nineties. With this in mind, but without a fully developed story in hand, he recklessly went ahead and had sets built of Rector's restaurant in New York City. He told Mae to come up with an idea that would marry the period with the romantic and evocative locale.

# Hanging In

This was the film for which Mae claimed that the entire plot came to her in a psychic flash, generated by what she called The Force. Its title was *Every Day's a Holiday*, and what The Force clearly failed to reveal was that it would be her feeblest film to date and her least successful at the box office.

On paper it was typical Mae West fare. The central character is Peaches O'Day, a confidence trickster who thinks nothing of selling the Brooklyn Bridge for a few bucks to any gullible passer-by. Her credo in life is 'keep a diary and someday it'll keep you'—a belief that several of her blackmailed suitors have found to be true. When a ruse involving a reform leader (Charles Winninger) backfires, Peaches hotfoots it to Boston and returns in a black wig as the famous French entertainer, Mademoiselle Fifi. The cast also included Charles Butterworth, Walter Catlett, and Herman Bing, with the romantic interest supplied by Edmund Lowe as New York's chief of detectives.

But *Every Day's a Holiday* just didn't add up to much, and nothing its star or its director, Eddie Sutherland, did altered the fact that with this one Mae had passed her 'sell by date.' Only a brief but welcome appearance by Louis Armstrong lived up to expectations. Indeed, the script was so inoffensive that, for the very first time, the British censors gave a Mae West movie a U certificate, thus allowing children to see it. There were only two lines in the entire screenplay they objected to, and both were pretty innocuous. 'I wouldn't lift my veil for that guy' was one, and 'I wouldn't let him touch me with a ten-foot pole' was the other.

The film, released in 1937, garnered mediocre reviews and, although it didn't lose money, its box office returns

# Mae West

Mae poses with the very popular Charlie McCarthy.

were minimal compared to the West offerings of three years earlier. Mae was suddenly branded box office poison but then so were, at one time or another, Katharine Hepburn, Joan Crawford, and Greta Garbo. Still, it must have been a bitter blow to her ego.

After a typically controversial—and rare—radio appearance to help promote *Every Day's A Holiday*, Mae found herself banned from the mighty NBC network for failing to exercise due discretion on *The Chase and Sanborn Hour*, a popular, live Sunday night entertainment hosted by ventriloquist Edgar Bergen, creator of Charlie McCarthy and Mortimer Snerd. Despite the fact that she was asked to tone down several suggestive intonations from an Adam and Eve sketch (written by Arch Oboler) which she and Don Ameche were to perform, she went ahead as she had intended to do all along and uttered the line 'Would you, honey, like to try this apple sometime?' in so come-hither a manner that outraged church groups across the country jammed the studio's switchboard with their protests. Mae did not make another radio appearance for twelve years.

Unrepentant, despite all the bad press she was receiving, she then traveled to New York where she put together a stage show for which she received $5,000 a week from Loew's State Theatre. Her latest movie may not have found favor with the public, nor her behavior with the bigwigs at NBC, but in person Mae was still a riot and she cleaned up in the city that had first bestowed stardom on her.

As far as Paramount was concerned, their one-time savior was now bad news. The combination of her ill judged behavior on *The Chase and Sanborn Hour*, plus the lukewarm-to-hostile reviews her last two movies had received

# Mae West

With W.C. Fields in *My Little Chickadee*, 1940.

had been decisive factors. Mae was to be released. Nor was there any joy from Emmanuel Cohen who, disappointed at the box office takings of *Goin' to Town* and *Every Day's a Holiday*, decided not to renew her contract with him either. Mae was on her own again. She was unable to find any takers for her *Catherine the Great* (which she hoped to shoot in Technicolor), and talk of starring opposite Clark Gable at MGM in a project provisionally called *New Orleans* also came to nothing.

In the fall of 1939, however, Mae was approached by Universal Pictures. Way back in 1915 while she was appearing in a show called *Such Is Life* in Los Angeles, she was introduced to Carl Laemmle, who founded Universal.

# Hanging In

With Joseph Calleia in *My Little Chickadee*, 1940.

## Mae West

From the collections of Roy Bishop and Harold Jacobs.

# Hanging In

The studio had just moved to large premises on Linkershim Boulevard, and Laemmle, always on the lookout for fresh new talent, considered signing her. But nothing came of it, and Mae returned to New York. In 1939 Laemmle was no longer in charge, having been ousted three years earlier. The studio was now run by Nate J. Blumberg and Cliff Work, both erstwhile executives at RKO. Their biggest star was Deanna Durbin, though Marlene Dietrich, who'd also recently quit Paramount, had just scored a success opposite James Stewart in Universal's hit remake of *Destry Rides Again*.

Blumberg and Work had an idea they hoped would prove box office dynamite: to cast Mae West and W. C. Fields (who had also been a Paramount star) opposite each other. The studio owned a property called *The Jaywalkers* which they thought might be the perfect vehicle. But both stars demurred, whereupon Mae went to work on an original idea she called *The Lady and the Bandit*. Fields approved of the finished treatment and the result was *My Little Chickadee*.

Set in the 1880s, it tells the story of a beauty called Flower Belle Lee (West) who, having become entangled with a masked gunman ('I was in a tight spot, but managed to wriggle out of it') finds herself in court. There, on being asked whether she is showing contempt, she answers 'No, I'm doing my best to hide it.' Forced out of town, she meets a medicine man called Cuthbert J. Twillie (Fields) who asks her what kind of a woman she is. 'Sorry,' comes the reply. 'I can't give out samples.' Believing Twillie to have money, Flower Belle contrives a fake marriage, sees him proclaimed sheriff of Greasewood City, charms all and sundry, and (like

# Mae West

Jimmy Stewart in *Destry Rides Again),* finishes up restoring law and order to the place. The film ends with Fields moving on to pastures new and inviting Mae to 'come up and see me sometime.'

Mae's own dialogue had its customary selection of one-liners ('I generally avoid temptation unless I can't resist it...' and 'I learned early that two and two are four and that five will get you ten if you know how to work it') but the movie, with all its comic potential, was never the classic it should have been. Mae and Fields were far too voluble as personalities to spend much time in the same frame, apart from which she made it clear from the outset that she totally disapproved of his drinking and would not tolerate him on the set if she smelled alcohol on his breath. For much of the movie's running time the two stars appear separately—which meant that the chemistry between them was minimal. Each was concerned that the other shouldn't receive the lion's share of the laughs, with the result that an uneasy air of contrivance permeates Eddie Sutherland's direction. Though Mae claimed her co-star wrote just one scene in the movie, he nonetheless received co-authorship credit.

Released in 1940, *My Little Chickadee* did well at the box office (without being a smash), but was not critically well received. One of the most condemnatory reviews came from Frank S. Nugent in the *New York Times.* Above a picture of Fields, not Mae, Nugent commented that 'Miss West's humor, like Miss West herself, seems to be growing broader with the years...' and referred to Fields as 'the innocent victim of someone else's bad taste.'

Nevertheless, the movie, which was modestly budgeted compared to some of Mae's earlier successes, did well

# Hanging In

*The Heat's On*, 1943.

enough for Universal to offer her a three picture deal. But neither party could agree on the projects, and Mae, who hadn't enjoyed her experience at the studio, declined. A possibility

## Mae West

From the collections of Roy Bishop and Harold Jacobs.

# Hanging In

A lobby card for *The Heat's On*, 1943, with Victor Moore.

of working with John Barrymore also came to naught; so did the suggestion of a remake of the 1929 *The Great Divide* for Warner Bros.

Instead of concentrating on rescuing her failing career, Mae became increasingly involved with spiritualism, especially after making the acquaintance of a well-known medium called T. Jack Kelly, who, in turn, introduced her to a woman who taught meditation. Mae's ultimate hope, of course, was to reach her beloved mother Tillie in a séance. Which, in time, she did.

Three years passed before Mae made another movie. She hit the headlines in a big way however when, in 1942, Britain's RAF pilots named their new life jackets 'Mae Wests,' prompting a delighted Mae to remark 'I've been in *Who's Who* and I know what's what, but it's the first time I've ever made the dictionary.'

## Mae West

In 1943 Mae was approached by director Gregory Ratoff (who, in his capacity as an actor had worked with her in *I'm No Angel*), to appear for Columbia Pictures in a film version of a Broadway musical called *Tropicana*. Because she clearly felt the time had come to get back into professional harness, she said yes. But she hadn't reckoned on the script—retitled *The Heat's On* and released in 1943—which was about a musical comedy star's involvement with a pair of crooked producers (played by Victor Moore and William Gaxton). It was a catastrophe and only a sense of loyalty to Ratoff kept her from pulling out of the inevitable debacle. With uncharacteristic honesty she admitted it was the biggest mistake of her professional life.

How could she know—except possibly through The Force—that her movie career had more or less come to an ignominious end?

# Chapter 6

# UPS and DOWNS

By 1944 Mae's relationship with Jim Timony had deteriorated badly. Though he was still in love with her, what little feeling she may have once had for him had evaporated completely. He continued to be her manager, but dogsbody would be a description nearer to the truth. Where once she relied absolutely on his judgment and wouldn't sign a document without his approval, she now used him to run errands and to make sure the more menial aspects of her day to day life ran smoothly. She even tried to remove him from the Ravenswood Apartments by suggesting he live in a bungalow behind a church hall she had turned into a small theatre. He wouldn't hear of it, though he did agree to run the theatre for her.

All too aware that he was no longer a vital adjunct to her life, Timony's frustration and his jealousy of rival suitors began to cause Mae real embarrassment. His constant spying on her represented an invasion of her precious privacy. Her sister Beverly and brother John spent most of their time taking care of the ranch and living off the generosity of their famous sibling whose numerous real estate deals around Los Angeles had made her an extremely wealthy woman.

Nineteen-forty-four was also the year in which Mae decided to make one more attempt at resuscitating her *Catherine the Great* project. Thanks to the disastrous reception given to *The Heat's On,* Hollywood no longer looked on her as a saleable commodity, and she knew she'd have to wait until the heat was off before resuming her movie career. But her success at Loew's State Theatre in New York convinced her that she still had a career on Broadway. With this in mind, she adapted her movie script of *Catherine the Great*, renamed it *Catherine Was Great*, and submitted it to Lee Shubert.

Shubert said yes, hiring Mike Todd to produce and Roy Hargrave to direct. After a standing-room-only pre-Broadway tryout at the Forrest Theatre in Philadelphia, the show moved to Broadway where it opened at the Shubert Theatre on 2 August, 1944.

Audiences loved Mae—especially her curtain speech: 'I'm glad you like my Catherine,' she told them, one hand characteristically on her hip, the other patting her wig. 'I like her too. She ruled thirty million people and had three thousand lovers. I do the best I can in two hours.' The critics, alas, were less charmed. Writing for *The Nation*, Joseph Wood Krutch rather pompously felt that 'we highbrows are going to have to give up the attempt to find something really significant in Mae.' In the New York *Daily News* John Chapman quipped 'I am afraid it will be a bust, which will

# Ups and Downs

Mae as Catherine the Great in *Catherine Was Great*, 1944.

give Miss West one more than she needs'; while Louis Kronenberger for *PM* also punned with 'Mae West slips on the steppes.' Most devastating of all, though, was *Time Magazine's* unsigned verdict: '[It has] the specific gravity of

# Mae West

lead, and the results, when not merely sedative, were often crushing.' *Catherine Was Great* played for 191 performances but failed to recoup its $150,000 investment. It toured Baltimore, Boston, Washington, Pittsburgh and, finally, Chicago. When it ended its run in May 1945, Mae had been on the road for almost a year—during which time she had also managed to do her bit for the war effort by appearing in military training films, and, more generously, by selling off some of her precious diamonds whose value she converted to war bonds.

Back in Los Angeles, and without so much as a whiff of a movie offer, Mae agreed to appear in a stage comedy for the Shuberts called *Ring Twice Tonight*. It was a topical subject, dealing, as it did, with Nazi agents, and the role she was offered was that of an FBI agent. As usual, Mae went to work on the script, changing much of her character's dialogue to suit her own well-tried personality. In the same spirit of tailor-made alteration, the play's title was also overhauled to *Come On Up, Ring Twice*. It opened in Long Beach, California in May 1946 prior to moving to San Francisco. But although an optimistic J. J. Shubert had booked a Broadway house, he changed his mind, deeming the piece not strong enough for New York or its knives-to-the-ready critics. With Mae West now no longer a reliable box office draw either in Hollywood or on Broadway, she would just have to peddle her talents elsewhere.

Mae's movies had always been popular in Britain, but, amazingly, she had never been out of America. The time had come for her to do some overseas traveling, and what better way to combine business with pleasure than to hit England with a show? And what better show than *Diamond Lil*?

# Ups and Downs

In August 1947, she and the omni-present Jim Timony boarded the *Queen Mary*. Disembarking onto British soil at Southampton, Mae West, in typical fashion, told reporters that the real reason she'd come to England was 'because of your men.' She was giving them the 'shtick' they clearly wanted to hear, though some accounts of her arrival indicate that a general air of disappointment prevailed because of her 'modest' appearance and general lack of flamboyance or sex appeal. She wore plain black dresses and practically none of her fabled jewelry. Clearly, if they wanted to see Mae West, Hollywood legend, they'd just have to wait until the show opened.

After checking into London's elite Savoy Hotel, Mae began auditions. She cast Bruno Barnabe (out of eighty hopefuls) to appear opposite her as the 'Latin Lover' Juarez, although she admitted he was too old for the part. His salary was forty pounds a week; she got two thousand. By all accounts, rehearsals were chaotic and disorganized—just as they had been twenty years earlier when Mae first took to Broadway as a playwright. Several of the female members of the cast found their leading lady's behavior unpleasant and unprofessional.

Produced by English impresarios Val Parnell and Tom Arnold and directed by Peter Glenville, *Diamond Lil* opened its tryout engagement at the Palace Theatre in Manchester. The house was full, but the praise from the critics was tepid. 'Mae West,' wrote the *Manchester Evening News* 'did not entirely succeed in projecting the forceful character so well known on the films. Though always colorful...she was sometimes inaudible.' Blackpool came next, and, after playing the Opera House there for six weeks, the show

# Mae West

moved on to Glasgow's Alhambra Theatre, thence to Birmingham, and, finally, London where it opened at the Prince of Wales Theatre on 24 January, 1948.

Mae gave a less than high-powered opening night performance and, as in Manchester, was often inaudible. The reviews were lukewarm to hostile. 'Diamond Lil is a fifteen minute vaudeville act, crudely and casually padded out to two hours,' wrote Eric Bennett of the *Sunday Express,* while Dick Richards in the *Sketch* felt 'a little of her technique goes a long way...her stock-in-trade remains the same, but its effect has gone.' Only Hannen Swaffer of *The People* (who was, like Mae, deeply interested in spiritualism) had a kind word to say for her. 'Diamond Lil, in the legendary person of Mae West, came to London last night—and conquered it,' he wrote. No wonder Mae always retained her admiration for him.

Though the Lord Chamberlain diluted parts of the show by demanding certain changes, the initial response was excellent and twice-nightly performances yielded healthy box office returns. But audiences steadily diminished, and *Diamond Lil* folded in the first week of May 1948 after a disappointing run of only three months. A week later, Mae once again boarded the *Queen Mary* and left England, never to return.

The now former star arrived back in Hollywood with nothing on the horizon except two irksome lawsuits. In the first, she was accused of plagiarizing material for *Catherine Was Great,* and was being sued for $100,000. In the second, she faced a breach of agreement suit concerning the London box office receipts of *Diamond Lil*. Fortunately the plagiarism case was thrown out of court, but Mae had to pay

# Ups and Downs

In *Diamond Lil*, 1947.

$21,000 as settlement for the second. Nothing, it appeared, seemed to be going right. Showing singular lack of judgment, she turned down the role of Norma Desmond in

## Mae West

*Sunset Blvd.* which director Billy Wilder offered to her. Unable, like the fictional Miss Desmond, to distinguish between fantasy and reality, Mae regarded Wilder's offer as an affront. The very idea that she should play a washed-up former screen goddess was quite unthinkable. As far as Mae was concerned, she was ageless. *Sunset Blvd.*, released in 1950, eventually went on to become a movie legend in itself, winning two Oscars (for its screenplay and music score) and revitalizing the career of another erstwhile screen goddess, Gloria Swanson.

Having rejected a role that might have won her an Oscar nomination, Mae decided to revive *Diamond Lil* in New York, trying it out first in New Jersey and then Philadelphia. It opened on Broadway at the Coronet Theatre, where Mae was proclaimed by Richard Watts Jr. in the *New York Post* as 'a legend and an institution,' and the play pronounced 'a modern classic.'

For the first time since becoming Mae's manager, Jim Timony was not with her in New York. Due to failing health, he decided to remain in California. Despite Mae's insistence that he had outserved his usefulness, she missed him and wanted him around, especially after a twisted ankle kept her out of the show. She had to make do instead with a new private secretary called Larry Lee who took care of her correspondence and daily chores.

Mae returned to *Diamond Lil* yet again in late 1949, and this time played to packed houses at the Phoenix Theatre. A lengthy coast-to-coast tour followed, beginning in Boston and ending in California in April, 1951. Prior to that, however, the show went on what was called a 'Subway' tour for eight weeks, playing theaters in several of New York's boroughs.

# Ups and Downs

The author Allan Lewis had a bit part in the touring production, playing a character called 'Da Champ.' When I spoke to him in London recently, Lewis told me:

> I wasn't much of an actor, but I was six-foot-three and looked the part. Mae gave me the once over, and said, 'He'll do. He'll do.' And I did, for eight weeks.
>
> The actor Steve Cochran had one of the lead roles, and at one point in the show he had to lift me up and carry me off stage. Well, he took one look at me and said he couldn't possibly do that. I was far too big. I was sure they were going to fire me. But Mae said to him 'Honey, I guess I've been paying you far too much. You're getting soft. Try harder.' He did and managed it without another word.
>
> Generally, though, Mae had very little contact with the rest of the cast. She arrived by limo, did the show, signed autographs for her fans, and left by limo. She never socialized. She didn't smoke or drink and ate only health foods long before it was fashionable to do so. Oats were what she seemed to eat most of. There was an occasion, I remember, when one of the girls in the show caught a bad cold. Suddenly there was a knock on her dressing room and the stage manager came in with a bowl of chicken soup for her—compliments of Miss West. But that was the only time I ever saw her take an interest in any of the cast.
>
> The other thing I remember was that just before she made her entrance, she seemed to drop twenty years in age. It was astonishing. She must

have been—what? 57 or 58 at the time—but on stage she looked like a woman in her thirties. And she had this uncanny knack of summing up an audience within minutes of stepping onto the stage. She had a genius for knowing just what kind of a crowd she had in, and her performance would vary accordingly from night to night. She was aware of everything that was going on. Nothing escaped her.

Though it was an extremely lucrative and ego-boosting public period for Mae, there was no real stability in her private life, nor any romance. Timony's absence affected her more than she would have believed possible, and when she finally returned to Los Angeles, she was distraught to see just how much his health had deteriorated and how old he was looking. One thing was sure—he was incapable of handling her affairs now. In the summer of 1952, she took it on herself to arrange a tour of *Come On Up, Ring Twice.* When she returned after the tour to Los Angeles, Jim's health was even worse. He was suffering from a heart condition, and what he needed was a far healthier environment than the Ravenswood Apartments could provide. To this end Mae bought a magnificent, twenty-three-room beach house on the Pacific Coast Highway in Santa Monica. Here he could get all the fresh air his doctor prescribed. Timony duly moved into the new mansion and was cared for by Mae and by her sister Beverly whose drinking problem had not improved over the years.

Mae continued to indulge her interest in spiritualism and even began writing a book about T. Jack Kelly, the medium who had come to mean so much in her life. It was

## Ups and Downs

Out on the town.

never finished. She also devoted time to her career, though the two projects that interested her most came to nothing. The first was a TV series, to be produced by her old friend and associate William Le Baron, called *Great Romances of History* in which, among others, she would take on Cleopatra

# Mae West

and also reprise her performance as Catherine the Great. The second was the possibility of playing opposite Marlon Brando in a screen version of the 1940s Rodgers and Hart musical *Pal Joey* which Billy Wilder was hoping to direct at Columbia. But Harry Cohn, Columbia's supremo, thought Mae far too old for the role (it finally went to Rita Hayworth) and, as a consequence, both Wilder and Brando bowed out.

Despite the good, clean Santa Monica air and the spiritual attention Mae continued to lavish on Jim Timony, his condition worsened and on 5 April, 1954, he died. For more than thirty years Mae had relied on his loyalty and support, and, in her own complex way, she had always loved him. His passing affected her profoundly. Timony's body was sent to New York, where, in the presence of his sister and a nephew, he was buried at Holy Cross Cemetery. The funeral took place without Mae, who was not invited to attend.

Grief-stricken over the loss of Jim, Mae continued to take comfort in spiritualism and, as always, in her work. Her newest venture was a nightclub act she hoped to take to Las Vegas. She was sixty-one years old.

The idea had come to Mae when she met Richard DuBois, a twenty-one-year old Mr. America. Given her lifelong partiality to musclemen, she devised an act in which she would be surrounded by Mr. America and eight other contenders for the title. Though Mae planned to hold the auditions herself (naturally), she hired Charles O'Curran, who was once married to Paramount superstar Betty Hutton, to take charge of the choreography. But teaching a group of

## Ups and Downs

A caricature by David Lee.

potential Mr. Universes how to dance was no easy matter (as choreographer Jack Cole had discovered the previous year when he surrounded Jane Russell with a group of hunks in a production number for *Gentlemen Prefer Blondes*). In the end professional dancers had been hired, and the muscle-men were retained only as decoration.

Apart from Mae, there was just one other woman in the show: veteran actress Louise Beavers who had played the black maid Pearl in *She Done Him Wrong*.

# Mae West

Mae was booked by the management of the Sahara Hotel for two weeks at a salary of $50,000. The forty-five-minute show opened in July 1954 and was a smash, matching Marlene Dietrich's crowd-pleasing appearance in the same room the previous year. From Mae's opening number, 'I Like to Do All Day What I Do All Night,' to her closing song ('Frankie and Johnny') Mae and her G-string clad boys were a sensation, 'invigorating even for jaded Las Vegas,' as *Time Magazine* put it. The show was a sell-out, and its star, who was given a diamond bracelet by the hotel's grateful owner, was invited back for a second engagement the following Christmas.

Mae's career had been revitalized overnight. Wherever the act toured—Chicago, Los Angeles, San Francisco—she broke records. Her biggest triumph was in New York where, for six weeks, she played to capacity houses at the prestigious Latin Quarter. She was earning $97,000 a week.

For the first time in years, her love life was blooming too. It was even rumored that she was slowly working her way through the eight musclemen, one of whom allegedly couldn't take the strain and finished up in a monastery. The story was picked up by the prurient *National Enquirer,* after which she found herself the subject of a *Confidential Magazine* exposé. *Confidential* claimed that in the mid-1950s Mae had had an affair with former boxer Chalky Wright, a Mexican Black she'd engaged as her chauffeur. They could also, had they so wished, have written about her affairs, over the years, with heavyweight boxing champions James J. Corbett, Joe Louis, and Jack Dempsey, entertainer Harry Richman, actors George Raft and Mike Mazurki, accordionist Guido Diero,

## Ups and Downs

boxer Johnny Indrisano, and escapologist Houdini—to name but a handful.

At any rate she sued the publication—and won. More unwelcome publicity came after Jayne Mansfield broke up her alleged affair with Hungarian-born Mickey Hargitay, who had become part of the musclemen act.

Her association with bodybuilders did result in one positive and fulfilling liaison. On her return to California, Mae met and fell for a thirty-two-year-old holder of the Mr. Baltimore title. He was Paul Novak, a merchant marine of Polish birth, and the attraction was mutual. Paul, who had also vied with Hargitay over Mae, became indispensable to her and was with her when she died.

When the musclemen tour ended, Mae cut an album for Decca called 'The Fabulous Mae West.' She then revived *Come On Up, Ring Twice,* this time casting Paul Novak as a newspaperman. The show toured successfully, after which she and Paul returned to California and moved into the Santa Monica beach house. There, in 1957, Mae decided—with a little help from her friends and a great deal of help from her secretary Larry Lee—to write her memoirs. It was a daunting task. So much had happened in her life that she wondered whether she'd be able to remember it all, especially as some vital memory-jogging documents that had been housed in the basement of the Ravenswood had been lost when the basement was flooded. Fortunately, her Hollywood years had been extensively documented by others, and, as she probably never had any intention of telling the complete truth about her formative years anyway, those memories she did retain would no doubt serve her well enough. After all, what she didn't know she could always invent...

Her method was to dictate the book to Lee, then make corrections and alterations on the manuscript. And although initially unsure whether she had undertaken more than she was ultimately able to deliver, her publisher, Prentice Hall, was extremely enthusiastic about the project. Soon, the more Mae dictated, the more involved she became.

She did take a break from writing when she was approached by producer Jerry Wald to appear on live television. Wald was producing the 1958 Academy Awards ceremony, and, as a surprise, wanted Mae to make an unbilled appearance singing Frank Loesser's 'Baby, It's Cold Outside' with Rock Hudson.

It was too good an opportunity to miss. The ceremony was held at Hollywood's Pantages Theatre, and, when the time came for Mae to appear, she made her entrance on a *chaise longue*, looking stunning. The number went beautifully, and Mae received a standing ovation from an audience that included Paul Newman, Fred Astaire, Maurice Chevalier, Gregory Peck, Doris Day, Clark Gable, Sophia Loren, Bette Davis, Gary Cooper, and her former co-star Cary Grant. She had lost none of her glamour or star quality, and this glittering gathering was happy to let her know it. The evening was just one more triumph for Mae West.

## Chapter 7

# BOWING OUT

In 1960, Mae adapted to her own specific requirements a typical French boulevard sex comedy about a much-married English socialite who enters matrimony for the sixth time. It was called *Sextette* (later changed to *Sextet*), and the author was Charlotte Francis. Initially the Shuberts were quite interested in it for Broadway, but when they finally said no, Mae presented it herself at the Edgewater Beach Playhouse in Chicago. The opening night was calamitous. Though suffering from a serious bout of laryngitis Mae appeared as scheduled, with the result that she only had a tenuous grip on her lines, and even the lines she remembered were inaudible. Although on opening night her fans rallied, the reviews were less generous.

To make matters worse, on the first Saturday of the run, Alan Marshall, who was playing her leading man, fell ill and although he managed to complete the matinee performance, he was unable to appear in the evening and the

# Mae West

show was cancelled. That same night he suffered a heart attack and died.

As there was no understudy, the stage manager deputized for the next few performances and went on carrying the script. By the end of the week Tom Conway, the brother of George Sanders, had been hired for the role, but he arrived in Chicago so drunk that Mae dismissed him on the spot. Another story has it that he took one look at the script and fled. Either way he never appeared in the show.

The role eventually went to a good-looking actor called Francis Bethencourt who gave Mae the performance she wanted. But to no avail. The Chicago run was a disaster the scale of which was reflected in the box office takings: a paltry $13,000 and the worst in the history of the Edgewater Beach Playhouse.

From Chicago the company moved to Detroit, then on to Warren, Ohio, one of whose critics felt that Mae was 'a good ad for retirement.' Their next date was Columbus, Ohio, where business improved slightly, thanks in the main to Mae's continual honing of the script. By adding several bits of typical Mae West 'shtick' and tailoring the role even further to suit the public's image of what they thought she ought to be, the play was in better shape and even received encouraging reviews.

The final engagement was the Coconut Grove Playhouse in Miami, and for the first time *Sextet* actually did terrific business. Audiences there loved the ageing star in it, and so did most of the critics. 'Like it or not, she's an American institution' was the verdict of one of the local reviewers, and to judge from the audience attendance figures the public agreed.

# Bowing Out

But it was too little too late. *Sextet* ended its tour showing a considerable financial loss and Mae returned to Los Angeles without much work in prospect. There was talk of several TV sitcom possibilities, none of which materialized, and the only professional satisfaction she had during this period of her life was cutting the occasional disc for Plaza Records.

For the most part, Mae 'rested,' dividing her time between her Ravenswood apartment and her Santa Monica beach house. Although sister Beverly and brother John would often come in from the ranch to spend time with her, her constant companion was Paul Novak, from whom she had become inseparable. He was always on hand to attend to her needs, to escort her when she went out, and to act as her bodyguard. He also made sure she ate the right foods and kept reasonably healthy, especially since she had recently been diagnosed as diabetic and was also suffering badly from cataracts. Without Paul, her life would probably have been shorter than it was, and her final years much less active and fulfilling.

She did, of course, maintain her interest in spiritualism. Since Jim Timony's death she'd longed to make contact with him 'on the other side,' but so far this had not happened. What she'd hoped was that Jim would continue to do in death what he had done in life: guide and advise her on her career.

A one-off TV appearance for producer Arthur Lubin proved a success. Lubin asked Mae to star in a show called *Mr. Ed* which, similar to the series of Francis the talking mule movies for Universal, was all about a talking horse.

# Mae West

The show was aimed primarily at children, and Lubin persuaded Mae to do it if only for the benefit of a young new audience which, in the main, would never have heard of her. Mae agreed, and the show, in which she played herself, was a great success; so much so that Lubin asked her whether she would consider playing a female detective in a weekly TV series he was developing. But she declined the offer on the grounds that episodic TV was too much work. Instead, she entered hospital (using her sister's name) for successful surgery on her cataracts.

Professionally speaking, not a great deal happened in Mae's life between 1963 and 1969. She was forced to liquidate some of her real estate to support herself, the increasingly inebriated Beverly, and her brother John who, sadly, died in 1967 at the age of sixty-four.

There were the usual discussions about projects that were destined never to materialize, typical of which was an operatic version of *Diamond Lil*. Movie producer Ross Hunter offered her the role of a madam in *The Art of Love*, but she turned it down when he insisted she accept guest star billing and refused to let her rewrite her part. (It was eventually played by Ethel Merman.) She did, however, continue to make records. The most successful of these was 'Way Out West,' an album of rock songs which contained Bob Dylan's 'If You Gotta Go,' The Beatles' 'Day Tripper,' and Percy Sledge's 'When a Man Loves a Woman.' She followed 'Way Out West,' which sold about 100,000 copies, with 'Wild Christmas,' and in 1968 was invited by the University of Southern California's film fraternity, Delta Kappa Alpha, to be the guest of honor at their thirtieth honorary awards banquet.

Bowing Out

LP record album cover for 'Wild Christmas.'

Sharing the program with her were James Stewart and director Mervyn LeRoy, and the co-chairmen of the event were directors George Cukor and Robert Wise. It was a glittering occasion, and Mae, who was dressed entirely in white and drenched in diamonds, dominated it completely. A series of well-chosen clips, followed by her entrance surrounded by a group of all-American football jocks, and, finally a rendition of 'Frankie and Johnny,' confirmed Mae's status as a living legend. To a standing ovation she quipped:

# Mae West

John Huston and Mae seated side by side at a banquet

'I want to thank you for your generous applause and your heavy breathing.'

The usual TV interest followed, including requests from all the best-known chat show hosts and an offer to appear on *The Red Skelton Show*, which she accepted. She also agreed to sign a deal with producer Robert Wise who wanted to star her in a big TV special. Unfortunately, Wise was unable to find the necessary sponsorship and the special never happened. Even in the late 1960s Mae's risqué persona gave cause for alarm.

It was producer Robert Fryer who found a way of bringing Mae West back to the medium in which she had

## Bowing Out

table during shooting of *Myra Breckinridge*, 1966.

achieved global celebrity and which had abandoned her for the last twenty-six years: the movies. He was producing, for Twentieth Century-Fox, Gore Vidal's controversial novel *Myra Breckinridge*, a best-seller about a transsexual film buff. He offered Mae the role of Letitia Van Allan, a lascivious talent agent. The initial sum of money suggested was $100,000 which Mae refused. She wanted $300,000. The studio dithered, then agreed. Their indecision cost them a further $50,000 and the deal was closed in July 1969 at $350,000. Mae was also given the freedom to rewrite her own part and an assurance that the character's name would be changed from Le*ti*tia to the less obvious Leticia. Her

# Mae West

director was a relative newcomer from England called Mike Sarne, an erstwhile pop star whose first movie, *Joanna*, about 'Swinging London' in the sixties, had become a cult success.

The *Myra Breckinridge* 'shoot' became big news, attracting journalists from all over the world. The actual star of the show was Raquel Welch, although there was no doubt in anyone's mind that Mae, who was playing a sex symbol at the unbelievable age of seventy-six, was the movie's centre of gravity publicity-wise. Inevitably there was talk of a personality clash between the two super-egos, with Mae referring to the gorgeous Raquel as 'that other woman.'

As shooting progressed, she grew increasingly hostile towards her. But the main problem experienced by the publicity department at Fox had less to do with the rivalry between West and Welch than with Raquel's impossible demands and uncooperative attitude towards the press. Because of director Sarne's relative inexperience, the movie went way over its budget (the final cost was three million dollars) and was brought to a perfunctory close when studio head Richard Zanuck, aware that he had a turkey on his hands, ordered Sarne to complete the film with what he had already shot.

The end result was a terrible mish-mash of both plot and style. Sarne resorted to restructuring the screenplay he co-wrote with David Giler and inserting clips from old Twentieth Century-Fox movies in an effort to make some kind of narrative sense of it all.

Mae didn't make her first appearance until the movie was well under way and, although she was undoubtedly

## Bowing Out

the best thing in it, much of her part—including a couple of production numbers and a great deal of dialogue deemed too risqué even in 1970—was lost to the cutting room floor. None of this prevented Mae from attracting the lion's share of interest when the show opened on 24 June, 1970 at New York's Criterion Theatre.

The critics had something to whinge about, and whinge they did, with Howard Thompson in the *New York Times* complaining that Mae had 'been done wrong by getting short shrift' in a movie that 'collapses like a tired, smirking elephant with no place to go.' The best *Variety* could muster (in a generally negative review) was that it was 'an interesting try at an elusive story.'

The film was an artistic and financial failure, but Mae came out of it well enough, given that so much of her material failed to survive the final edit. She had also proved that she was still big news and still had a following.

As was usually the case after each of Mae's 'comeback' appearances, she enthusiastically set about working on several projects that were destined never to happen, such as the possibility of a Technicolor remake of *Diamond Lil* to be directed by George Cukor.

She had to wait until 1973 before her next professional engagement. This time it was MGM that approached her—not to make a movie, but an album of rock songs to be called 'Great Balls of Fire.' At the age of eighty Mae West found herself sitting at a microphone recording her unique versions of 'Rock Around the Clock' and 'Whole Lot of Shakin' Goin' On.'

A couple of years later, and with much assistance from her secretary Larry Lee, she brought out a novelized version

# Mae West

of *Pleasure Man*. She also hoped to cash in on the success of Mart Crowley's gay play *The Boys in The Band*, as well as the many other homosexual-themed plays being produced at the time—by novelizing *The Drag*. But it never happened. In 1975 she did manage to complete one more book, a nonfiction tome called *On Sex, Health, and* ESP. But it was not nearly as good as her autobiography, and, in truth, should never have been published.

The following year, chat-show host Dick Cavett invited her to appear on a TV special for CBS called *Back Lot USA*. For a fee of $25,000 she would be expected to sing a couple of songs (she chose 'After You've Gone' and 'Frankie and Johnny') and be interviewed 'live.' Though she wasn't particularly happy about the idea, she agreed and, despite some tense moments on the set, she managed, with the help of the ever-present Paul Novak, to become the only highlight in a show the *Daily News* dismissed as a 'catastrophe.' The *New York Times* concurred: 'Cavett's Show Flounders until Mae West' was the headline under which its critic wrote '[Mae West]) is something—a wonderful, glamorous, talented and marvelously witty something—unto herself.'

Her successful appearance on the show again stimulated interest in the 'ageless' Mae West and resulted in a screen version of her play *Sextet*. It was to be the indomitable star's last professional appearance.

She had been trying to get the project off the ground for some time, and it looked as though she might be successful when MGM showed an interest in it. But a change of management at the studio scuppered the idea. Next, Warner Bros. said they were interested. But not very, it seemed, for they, too, decided to pass. Then, just when it

# Bowing Out

*Sextette*, 1978, with an all-star cast.

## Mae West

looked hopeless, two wealthy young men, Daniel Briggs, aged twenty-one, and Robert Sullavan, aged twenty-three, came up with the necessary finance. The film was called *Sextette* (reverting to the play's original French title) and the director was Irving Rapper, a seventy-nine year-old Hollywood studio veteran who, way back in 1942, had directed Bette Davis and Paul Henreid in *Now, Voyager*. Timothy Dalton was chosen as Mae's leading man, and the rest of the cast included Tony Curtis, George Hamilton, Dom DeLuise, Ringo Starr, and Walter Pidgeon, plus George Raft who had helped launch Mae's movie career with *Night After Night*. The costume designer Mae hired was another Hollywood veteran, Edith Head, winner of eight Academy Awards. Understandably, the press had a field day. At the venerable age of eighty-three Mae West was returning to the screen in the starring role of a sexpot who puts the make on half-a-dozen hunks. Could this possibly be happening? It certainly was, though when the cameras finally rolled, Irving Rapper decided the circus wasn't for him. He was replaced by the English director Ken Hughes, whose track record included *Chitty Chitty Bang Bang* and *The Trials of Oscar Wilde*.

Filming officially began at Paramount Studios (the star's alma mater) on 2 December, 1976. To mark the occasion, a banner was draped across the imposing Paramount gates that read 'Welcome Home, Mae West.'

All too soon, however, Hughes realized he had his work cut out. Mae could barely remember two consecutive lines and had to have a small receiving device attached to her ears through which her dialogue was fed. Nor could she remember her moves or any bits of business she had been

## Bowing Out

given. Even walking became a physical impossibility for her, and often she had to be lifted bodily off the ground by whoever was sharing the scene with her to be conveyed from one point to another on the set. On one occasion Hughes shot a particular scene seventy-five times before Mae got it right.

Many of the movie's best lines were filched from her earlier successes, though several new additions to the West repertoire were introduced. When Timothy Dalton tells her he's British and has a stiff upper lip, she replies 'Well, you've gotta start somewhere.' To one of the athletes on parade she says, 'I'd sure like to see your javelin...'

The nightmare shoot finally ended in April 1977. Yet, despite all the publicity and interest the movie generated, it was deemed unreleasable and could not find a distributor. The following year *Sextette's* two young producers leased the Cinerama Dome in Hollywood for four weeks and, at a cost of $42,000 per week, (initially) released the movie themselves.

Though many of the reviewers praised Mae's un-doubted fortitude and bravery, the film itself was panned. A typical assessment was delivered by *Time Magazine*: '...a work so bad, so ferally innocent, that it is good, an instant classic...Mae West is her own best invention.' The acid-tongued Rex Reed, who had appeared in *Myra Breckinridge*, and about whose performance Mae refused to comment, had this to say of her: '...the hip grinding is arthritic and the voice...sounds like an old cat having a bad dream...she looks like something they found in the basement of a pyramid. Even those who enjoy Mae West films from the vaults are going to find this one hard to take.'

# Mae West

Tony Curtis with Mae in *Sextette*, 1978.

*Sextette* eventually found a distributor in Crown-International. They booked it into the Warfield Theatre in San Francisco where it opened on 16 November, 1978. Mae made a personal appearance and attracted 2,000 fans.

# Bowing Out

But the run was not successful. The movie was far too much of a camp curiosity to find favor with anyone other than dyed-in-the-wool Mae West fans. Still, she returned to Los Angeles with the San Francisco opening-night ovation still ringing in her cars.

It was the very last time she would hear that cherished sound of approbation she so desperately needed. A week before she was due to celebrate her eighty-seventh birthday, and after experiencing periods of disorientation, Mae fell out of bed and suffered a concussion. She was taken by Paul Novak to the Good Samaritan Hospital where it was discovered she had had a mild stroke. Although she occasionally rallied and was able to take brief walks with Paul up and down the hospital corridors, her strength was giving out.

When the hospital authorities said there was little more they could do, Paul brought her back to her Ravenswood apartment where she died on 22 November, 1980 after having had the last rites administered by a Catholic priest. Two days later, George Raft died.

A private memorial service was held for 100 close friends on 25 November at the Old North Church, Forest Lawn. An additional note of sadness was added by the appearance of her inebriated sister Beverly who was too distressed to enter the church. Her eulogy, written by Kevin Thomas and delivered by producer Ross Hunter, concluded, "Mae West figured that in one way or another she would live forever. And she probably will." She was subsequently entombed in the family mausoleum at Cypress Hills Abbey in Brooklyn, New York.

# Mae West

In her will, Mae left Beverly (who died in 1982) $25,000, her limousine, and her personal effects, including her jewelry. Paul and her secretary Larry were each left $10,000. The rest of her fortune was divided between friends and relatives. The Santa Monica beach house had been sold prior to Mae's death, but not the ranch which, for some years had been in a bad state of disrepair. It soon became derelict and was ransacked by squatters.

Where most of Hollywood's other screen goddesses handed over their personas to the studio for molding and refining, Mae West arrived fully packaged and entirely of her own creating. To some, she started off as a parody of the *femme fatale*—the predatory man-eater who always ensnared her prey. As she continued to perpetuate this image over the years, to many she became something of a joke. There were even rumors, as mentioned before, that she was actually a man in drag.

She may indeed have been a threat to the Legion of Decency and the proverbial thorn in the side and scourge of the world's censors, but because she was so larger than life and refused to take herself seriously, she was no threat to her millions of female fans who were as intrigued by her in-your-face sexuality and exaggerated mannerisms as they might be by a brilliant female impersonator. And although she ended up as a parody of herself, no one—not even Dietrich or Garbo—had so unswerving an image of herself as did this 'empress of sex.'

From the start of her career to its finish, Mae West projected a vision of sensuality that was unique in Hollywood's

## Bowing Out

history. And because she believed so implicitly in the legend she had invented for herself, she was able, at the age of eighty-three, to play a sex object and almost get away with it. Not for her the mothers, grandmothers, maiden aunts, or grotesques which many of her peers, such as Bette Davis, Joan Crawford, Joan Bennett, Sylvia Sidney, Katharine Hepburn, Mary Astor, or Myrna Loy resorted to playing in old age.

Mae West was always Mae West, the high priestess of glamour, and she spent a lifetime strengthening the courage of that conviction. In so doing, she became one of the great screen originals. There has never been anyone like her. Nor will there ever be. She was one of a kind.

# Mae West

# INDEX

**Boldface** indicates illustration.

*A La Broadway* 22, 23, 25, 31, 47
Academy Awards ceremony 110
Adams, Maud 32
'After You've Gone' 120
*Albatross, The* (later *Sex*) 31, 32
Alhambra Theatre, Glasgow 100
Alvin Reynolds Company 16
Ameche, Don 85
'Any Kind of Man' 27
Armstrong, Louis 83
Arnold, Tom 99
*Art of Love, The* 114
Austin, Gene 77
*Babe Gordon* (later *The Constant Sinner*) 41
'Baby, It's Cold Outside' 110
*Back Lot USA* 120
Banton, Travis 53, 55, 64, 65
Barnabe, Bruno 99
Barrymore, Ethel 37, 38
Barrymore, John 32, 37, 93
Beavers, Louise 107
*Belle of the Nineties* **62–69**
Bennett, Eric 100
Bergen, Edgar 85
Bethencourt, Francis 112
Biltmore Theatre, NYC 40
Bing, Herman **82**
Bishop, Roy **24, 28, 30, 39, 54, 73, 88, 92**
Blumberg, Nate J. 89
*Boys in the Band, The* 120
Brando, Marlon 106
Breen, Joseph 62

Breen Office 66, 74
Brentano, Lowell 56, 57
Briggs, Daniel 122
Bright, John 50
Brown, Johnny Mack **63**
Burkan, Nathan 40
Butterworth, Charles 83
Calleia, Joseph **87**
*Captive, The* 34
Catherine the Great 82, 97, 106
*Catherine the Great* (script) 86, 96
*Catherine Was Great* 96, **97**–98;
    plagiarism lawsuit 100
Catlett, Walter 83
Cavett, Dick 120
CBS TV (Columbia Broadcasting System) 120
Chapman, John 96
*Chase and Sanborn Hour, The* 85
Cinerama Dome, Hollywood 123
Clarendon, Hal 16
Cochran, Steve 103
Coconut Grove Playhouse, Miami 112
Cohen, Emmanuel 74, 77, 79, 86
Cohn, Harry 106
Cole, Jack 107
Columbia Pictures 94, 106
*Come On Up, Ring Twice* 98, 104, 109
*Confidential Magazine* 108
*Constant Sinner, The* (book and play) 41

# Mae West

Conway, Tom 112
Cook and Lorenz 22
Corbett, James J. 108
Coronet Theatre, NYC 102
Criterion Theatre, NYC 119
Crowley, Mart 120
Crown-International 124
Cuckor, George 115, 119
Cummings, Constance 45
Curtis, Tony 122, **124**
Dalton, Timothy 122, 123
Daly's Theatre, New York 32, 34
*Daredevil Jack* 29
Davis, Wilva 35
Delta Kappa Alpha 114
DeLuise, Dom 122
Dempsey, Jack 29, 108
'Diamond Lil' (song) **30**
*Diamond Lil* (stage play) 6, 37, **38**, **39**, 40, 41, 49; London production 98, 100, **101**; censorship by the Lord Chamberlain 100; lawsuit 100; discussion of opera version 114; possible film version 119. See also *She Done Him Wrong*.
Diero, Guido 108
Doelger, Jacob (maternal grandfather) 13
Dolly Sisters 25
Dowell, George B. 72, 74
*Drag, The* 33, 34, 40, 120
DuBois, Richard (Mr. America) 106
Durbin, Deanna 89
*East Lynne* 16
'Easy Rider' **39**
Edgewater Beach Playhouse, Chicago 111, 112

Eisner, Edward 32, 33, 34
Elite, The 27
Ellington, Duke 66
Empire Theatre, NYC 34
*Every Day's a Holiday* 10, **67**, **82**–84, 85
'Ev'rybody Shimmies Now' **24**
Eysler, Edward 23
'Fabulous Mae West, The' (LP album) 109
*Fatal Wedding, The* 16
Fields, W.C. **8**, 16, **86**, 89
Fifth Avenue Theatre, NYC 25
Folies Bergère 22, 23
Forest Lawn Cemetery 125
Forrest Theatre, Philadelphia 96
Francis, Charlotte 111
'Frankie and Johnny' **54**, 108, 120
Friml, Rudolf 27
Fryer, Robert 116
Gable, Clark 86
Gabriel, Gilbert W. 40
Gaxton, William 94
George, Gladys 79, 80
Girard Brothers 25
Glenville, Peter 99
*Go West Young Man* 80, **81**, 82
*Goin' to Town* 72, **73**, 74, 86
*Goodness Had Nothing to Do with It* (autobiography) 22, 36, 61, 79, 120
Gotham Theatre, Brooklyn 16
Grant, Cary **50**, **58**
*Graphic, The* 32
'Great Balls of Fire' (LP album) 119
*Great Divide, The* 93
*Great Romances of History* (proposed TV series) 105

# Index

Guinan, Texas 29, 45, 49
Hall, Mordaunt 60
Hamilton, George 122
Hammerstein, Arthur 27
Hargitay, Mickey 7, 8, 109
Hargrave, Roy 96
Hathaway, Henry 80
Hays Office 50, 52, 61
Hays, Will H. 50
Hayworth, Rita 106
'He's a Bad Man' **73**
Head, Edith 65, 122
*Heat's On, The* **91, 92, 93,** 94, 96
'Hello, Mi Amigo' **92**
Hogan, Willie 19
*Hollywood Reporter* 8, 9
Holy Cross Cemetery 106
Houdini, Harry 109
Howard, Gertrude 58
Huber, Harold **76**
Hudson, Rock 110
Hughes, Ken 122
Hunter, Ross 114
Huston, John **116**
'I Like to Do All Day What I Do All Night' 108
*I'm No Angel* 3, 6, 57–61, 94
'I Never Broke Nobody's Heart When I Said Goodbye' **28**
Indrisano, Johnny 109
*It Ain't No Sin* (later *Belle of the Nineties*) 62
Jacobs, Harold **24, 28, 30, 39, 54, 73, 88, 92**
Jarno, Raymond 35
*Jaywalkers, The* (*My Little Chickadee*) 89
Jolson, Al 23, 26, 43
Kearns, Jack 29

Kelly, T. Jack 93, 104
*Klondike Annie* 74–79
Kronenberger, Louis 97
Krutch, Joseph Wood 96
*Lady and the Bandit, The* (later *My Little Chickadee*) 89
Laemmle, Carl 86, 89
Larrimore, Francine 27
Lasky, Jesse L. 22, 23, 44, 45
Latin Quarter, NYC 108
Laughlin, Harry 25
Le Baron, William 22, 23, 31, 44, 45, 47, 57, 66, 74, 77, 105
Lee, David **107**
Lee, Larry (secretary) 102, 109, 119, 125
Legion of Decency 55, 61, 126
Leonard, Maurice 14
LeRoy, Mervyn 115
Lewis, Allan 103
life jacket 'Mae West' 93
Loesser, Frank 110
Loew's State Theatre, NYC 85, 96
Louis, Joe 108
Lowe, Edmund 83
Lubin, Arthur 113, 114
Lubitsch, Ernst 77, 79
Madden, Owney 32, 37, 45
'Mae West' life jacket 93
Majestic Theatre, Chicago 27
*Manchester Evening News* 99
Mansfield, Jayne 7, 8, 109
Marshall, Alan 111
Mast, Jane (pseudonym) 32, 33
Mayo, Archie 45
Mazurki, Mike 108
McCarey, Leo 63, 66
McCarthy, Charlie **84,** 85

131

# Mae West

McLaglen, Victor **75**
Merman, Ethel 114
MGM (Metro-Goldwyn-Mayer) 86, 119, 120
Michael, Gertrude 58, 60
Miljan, John 63, 66
*Mimic World, The* 29
Moore, Victor **93,** 94
Morgan, Marion 72, 74
Morgenstern, C. William 32, 33, 34
*Motion Picture Herald* 82
Mr. America 106
Mr. Ed (TV appearance) 113
Mr. Universe 7, 107
*Mrs. Wiggs of the Cabbage Patch* 16
*My Little Chickadee* **8,** 9, **86, 87,** 89, 90
*Myra Breckinridge* 14, 65, **117,** 118, 123
*Nation, The* 96
*National Enquirer* 108
National Legion of Decency — see Legion of Decency
NBC (National Broadcasting Company) 85
New Century Theatre, NYC 29
New London Theatre, New London, CT 32
*New York Daily Mirror* 32
New York *Daily News* 96, 120
*New-York Evening Post* 40
New York *Evening Telegram* 38
*New York Evening World* 23
*New York Herald* 23
*New York Herald Tribune* 32, 79, 80
*New York Post* 80, 102

*New York Times* 23, 38, 60, 74, 79, 90, 119, 120
*New York Tribune* 23
*New Yorker* 38
*Night After Night* **44,** 45, **46,** 47, **48,** 49, 122
North, Sheree 7
Novak, Paul 109, 113, 120, 125
Nugent Frank S. 90
O'Curran, Charles 106
O'Neill, Bobby 25
Oboler, Arch 85
'Occidental Woman in an Oriental Mood for Love' 77
*On Sex, Health, and ESP* 120
Opera House, Bayonne, NJ 33
Opera House, Blackpool 99
*Pal Joey* 106
Palace Theatre, Manchester 99
Pantages Theatre, Hollywood 110
Paramount Pictures 4, 16, 22, 44, 45, 49, 53, 55, 62, 69, 70, 77, 79, 85, 89, 106, 122
Paramount Theatre, NYC 74
Parnell, Val 99
*People, The* 101
Perry, Margaret 80
*Personal Appearance (Go West Young Man)* 79
Phoenix Theatre, NYC 102
'Piccolo' 25
Pidgeon, Walter 122
Plaza Records 113
*Pleasure Man* (play) 40, 41
*Pleasure Man* (novel) 120
*PM* (magazine) 97
Poli's Park Theatre, Bridgeport, CT 33

# Index

Prentice Hall 110
Prince of Wales Theatre, London 100
Princess Theatre, NYC 34
Production Code 62
Pryor, Roger **62,** 66
*Queen Mary,* the 99, 100
RAF (Royal Air Force) 93
Raft, George (Rauft) **44,** 45, 49, 108, 122, 125
Rapper, Irving 122
Ratoff, Gregory 58, 94
Ravenswood Apartments 2, 5, 12, 47, 69, 95, 104, 109, 113, 125
*Red Skelton Show, The* 116
Reed, Rex 123
Richards, Dick 100
Richman, Harry 26, 108
Riley, Lawrence 79
*Ring Twice Tonight* (later *Come On Up, Ring Twice*) 98
RKO Studios 45, 89
'Rock Around the Clock' 119
Rodgers and Hart 106
Roland, Gilbert 53
Royale Theatre, NYC 37, 42
Ruggles, Wesley 57
Sahara Hotel, Las Vegas 108
Sarne, Mike 14, 118
Savoy Hotel, London 99
Scott, Randolph 80
*Sex* 32, 34, 40, 45
*Sextet* (play, previously *Sextette*) 111–113, 120
*Sextette* (film) **121–124**
*She Done Him Wrong* 50, 52, 53, 55, **56,** 61. See also *Diamond Lil.*

Sheil, Bishop Bernard 55
Sherman, Lowell 50, 53
Shubert brothers 23, 32, 98, 111
Shubert, J. J. 29, 41, 98
Shubert, Lee 23, 96
Shubert Theatre, NYC 96
Skelton, Red 116
Skipworth, Alison 45
Snerd, Mortimer 85
*Sometime* 27
spiritualism 15, 93, 100, 104, 106, 113
Starr, Ringo 122
Stewart, James 115
*Such Is Life* 86
Sullavan, Robert 122
*Sunday Express* 1, 100
*Sunset Blvd.* 102
Sutherland, Edward 'Eddie' 83, 90
Swaffer, Hannen 6, 100
Technicolor 86, 119
*Ten Nights in a Bar Room* 16
*That St. Louis Woman* (later *Belle of the Nineties*) 62
Thew, Harvey 50
Thompson, Harlan 57
*Time Magazine* 97, 108, 123
Timony, James A. 'Jim' 26, 29, 32, 34, 40, 41, 47, 69, 72, 95, 99, 102, 104, 106, 113; illness 104; death 106.
Tinney, Frank 25
Todd, Mike 96
*Tropicana* 94
Twentieth Century-Fox 117, 118
*Uncle Tom's Cabin* 16
United Artists 45
Universal Pictures 86, 89, 91, 113

# Mae West

University of Southern California 114
*Variety* 25, 27, 32, 33, 74, 119
*Vera Violetta* 23
Vidal, Gore 117
*Virgin Man, The* 34
Wald, Jerry 110
Wallace, Frank (husband) 19–21, 71
Wallace, James Garrett 40
Walsh, Raoul 77
Warfield Theatre, San Francisco 124
Warner Bros. 43, 93, 120
Watts, Richard Jr. 102
'Way Out West' (LP album) 3, 114
Wayburn, Ned 17, 22
Welch, Raquel 118
West, Beverly (sister) 17, 25, 34, 37, 41, 47, 69, 96, 104, 113; death 125
West, John 'Jack' (brother) 41, 69, 96; death 114
West, John 'Battling Jack' (father) 14, 16, 41; death 71
West, Katie (sister) 13
West, Mae—birth 13; childhood training 15; childhood school 17; marriage 20–22; discovering jazz 27; plagiarism suit 32; autobiography 22, 36, 61, 79, 109, 120; prosecutions for indecency 34, **35**, **36**, 40;

San Fernando Valley hacienda 69, 96, 126; Santa Monica beach house 104, 109, 113, 126; real estate investments 96, 114; book on T. Jack Kelly 104; *On Sex, Health, and ESP*, 120; TV 105, 113, 114, 116, 120; spiritualism 15, 93, 100, 104, 106, 113; war effort 98; radio appearance 85; performing in England, 98–100; death and burial 125
West, Matilda Delker Doelger - 'Tillie' (mother) 13, 14, 15, 16, 17, 19, 20, 26, 34, 93; death 41
'Whole Lot of Shakin' Goin' On' 119
*Wicked Age, The* 34
'Wild Christmas' 114, **115**
Wilder, Billy 102, 106
William, Warren 80
'Willie of the Valley' **88**
Winninger, Charles 83
*Winsome Widow, A* **24**, 25
Wise, Robert 115, 116
Work, Cliff 89
Wright, Chalky 108
Wynn, Ed 27
Yablonsky, Lewis 45
*Ziegfeld Follies* 23
Ziegfeld, Florenz 17, 23, 25, 26
Zukor, Adolph 44, 45, 47, 49, 56

Photo by ian cook.

# Clive Hirschhorn

Born in South Africa, film and theatre critic Clive Hirschhorn worked for the London *Daily Mail* and London *Sunday Express*, contributing over 300 interviews to the latter and writing its prestigious 'Meeting People' column. In the late 1990s he edited the monthly London/New York theatre magazine *Applause*.

He is the author of *Gene Kelly: A Biography* (London, W.H. Allen, 1974, and U.S., Henry Regnery, 1975, updated in 1986 by St. Martin's Press); *The Films of James Mason* (LSP Books, 1976, and Citadel, 1977); and *The Warner Bros. Story* (1978, Octopus Books, U.K., and Crown, U.S.). Octopus and Crown also published the best-selling *The Hollywood Musical* (1981), followed by *The Universal Story* (1983, updated in 2000) and *The Columbia Story* (1989, updated in 1999). In 1987, he ghosted Lord Grade's memoir *Still Dancing*, published by Harper Collins. Clive Hirschhorn has homes in London and West Sussex, and regularly contributes to theater-oriented publications both in the U.K. and the U.S.